120+ SIG WORDS

PRACTICE PAGES

Kate likes **to** study.

Trace the word:

to

Write the word:

Color the pizza slices that have the word "**to**"

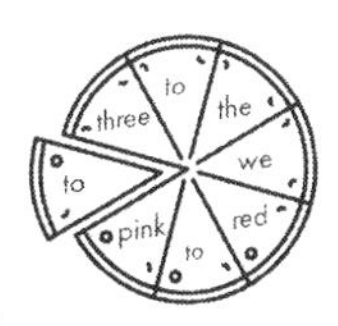

Find and circle the word "to"

Fill in the missing letters

Kate like

Write your own sentence using th

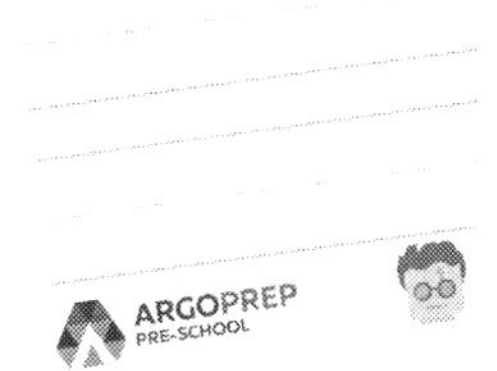

I **saw** a plane fly in the air.

Trace the word:

saw

Write the word:

Fill in the missing letters to make the word "saw"

_aw s_w

_a_ __w

___ s__ ___

fly in the air.

We are happy.

Trace the word:

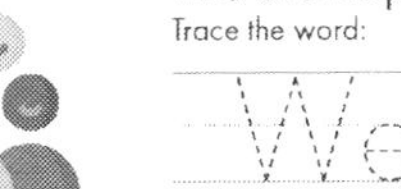

Write the word:

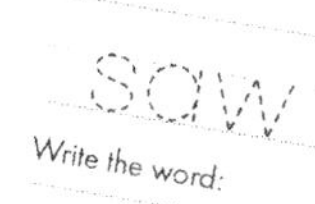

Color the pizza slices that have the word "**we**"

Let's work on our cutting and pasting skills. Cut out the word "**We**" from page 111 and paste it in the square box below to complete the sentence. Then read the sentence aloud!

Write your own sentence using the word **we**:

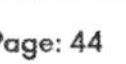

At ArgoPrep we believe in creating smart learning solutions so that every student can succeed in life.

We would love to hear your honest feedback and review of our workbooks on Amazon.

Want weekly BONUS & FREE Tracing worksheets?

Visit our website at **www.argoprep.com/tracing** to download and print more awesome tracing worksheets for your child.

ISBN: 978-1946755148
Published by ArgoPrep, Inc.

Aknowlegments:
Icons made by Freepik, Smashicons, Nikita Golubev Pixel Buddha, Good Ware, Pause08, mynamepong, DinosoftLabs, Vectors Market,turkkub, Those Icons Nikita Golubev, Roundicons, Twitter from www.flaticon.com

Don't forget to check out ALL our workbooks for preschoolers by **ArgoPrep!**

We believe in providing smart learning solutions so that every students can succeed in life.

SIGHT WORDS COVERED

I have **a** cat.
I see a circle **and** a square.
The bird is flying **away**.
This is a **big** house.
Mike's shirt is **blue**.
Can I go to the park?
Can Sarah **come** to the park with us?
Can you write **down** your name?
I **need** to find my shoes.
This table is too small **for** me.
She is very **funny**!
We will **go** to the museum.
I need **help** with my homework.
Tom will be **here** any minute.
I want to be an astronaut.
I live **in** New York City.
My mom **is** the best!
It is hot today.
Can I **jump** in the pool?
It is a **little** cold today.
Look at the beautiful mountain!
Can I **make** a cake?
My parents love **me**.
My teacher is smart.
The door does **not** open.
I have **one** brother.
I can **play** the guitar.
My favorite color is **red**.
She can **run** very fast.
She **said** goodbye.
I **see** a car.
The light is bright.
I have **three** siblings.
Kate likes **to** study.
There are **two** plants.
The sun is **up**.
We are happy.
Where are you from?
The banana is **yellow**.
You look tired.
We are **all** family.
I **am** hungry.
How **are** you?
I am **at** school.
We **ate** some apples.
I will **be** right back.
He has **black** shoes.
The rug is **brown**.
I want to play in the park **but** it's raining.
My friend **came** over to my house.
Did you finish your homework?
Do you know how to bake?
I like to **eat** carrots.
My sister is **four** years old.
I usually **get** up at eight.
This tastes **good**!
Do you **have** a dog?
He is very smart.
I put my pants **into** the washing machine.
I **like** to dance.
You **must** wear a jacket in the winter.

My mom gave me a **new** computer.
There is **no** thunder today.
Can I go to the zoo **now**?
I play soccer **on** Sundays.
Jamie wants to come to **our** party.
The bedroom lights are **out**.
Can we **please** go outside?
That dress is **pretty**!
She **ran** to catch the bus.
I **ride** my bike to school.
I **saw** a plane fly in the air.
Say cheese!
She wants to eat.
I am **so** full!
Can we leave **soon**?
That is a rocket.
There is a hole in this sock.
They want to take the train.
This is my notebook.
I am **too** tired to exercise.
The pencil is **under** the table.
Do you **want** to visit Italy?
John **was** excited for the trip.
She can sing very **well**.
Robert **went** to the dentist.
What time is it?
The bedroom ceiling is **white**.
Who is coming to the museum?
Will you help me?
I agree **with** you.

Yes, I got an A+.
I will eat **after** I finish my homework.
Can you repeat that **again**?
I have **an** idea.
There isn't **any** bread left.
I'm busy **as** a bee.
Can I **ask** a question?
I need to be home **by** seven.
I wish I **could** swim.

ARGOPREP
PRE-SCHOOL

LET'S BEGIN OUR **JOURNEY TO** RECOGNIZE AND LEARN **SIGHT WORDS.**

I have **a** cat.

Trace the word:

Write the word:

Color the pizza slices that have the word "**a**"

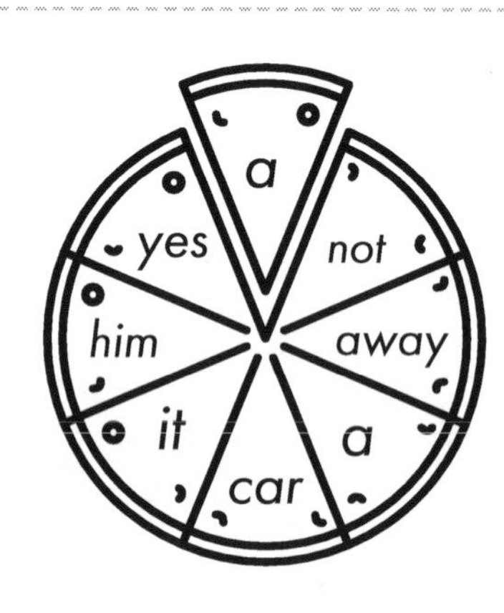

Let's work on our cutting and pasting skills. Cut out the letter "**a**" from page 111 and paste it in the square box below to complete the sentence. Then read the sentence aloud!

I have ☐ cat.

Write your own sentence using the word **a**:

I see a circle **and** a square.

Trace the word:

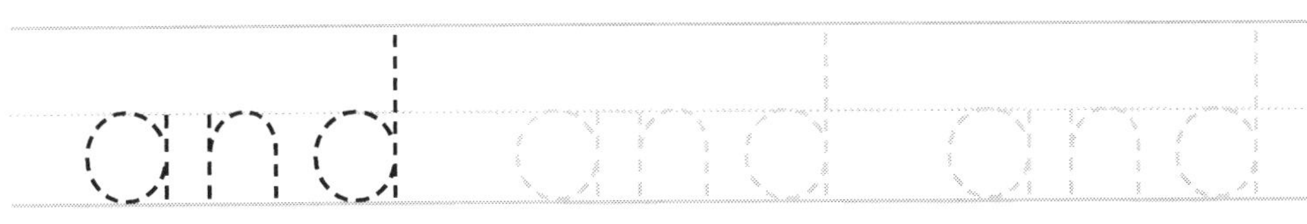

Write the word:

Color the puzzle pieces that have the word "**and**"

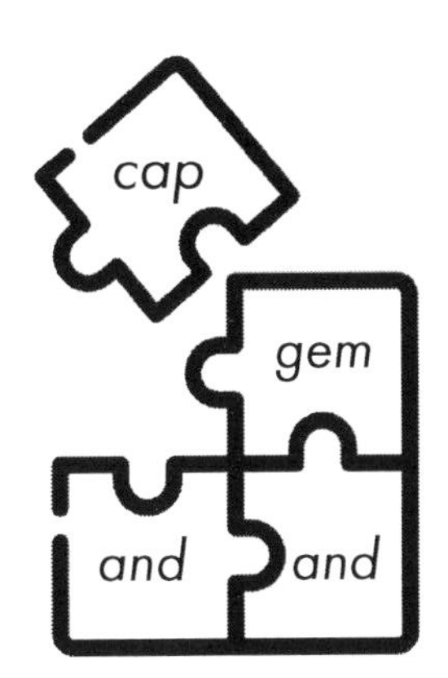

Find and circle the word "**and**"

y	n	v	z	l
m	t	x	a	x
w	o	s	n	w
u	m	b	d	q
g	c	n	n	d

Fill in the missing letters to make the word "**and**"

_nd **a_d**

an_ **_nd**

an_ **___**

I see a circle _ _ _ a square.

Write your own sentence using the word **and**:

The bird is flying **away**.

Trace the word:

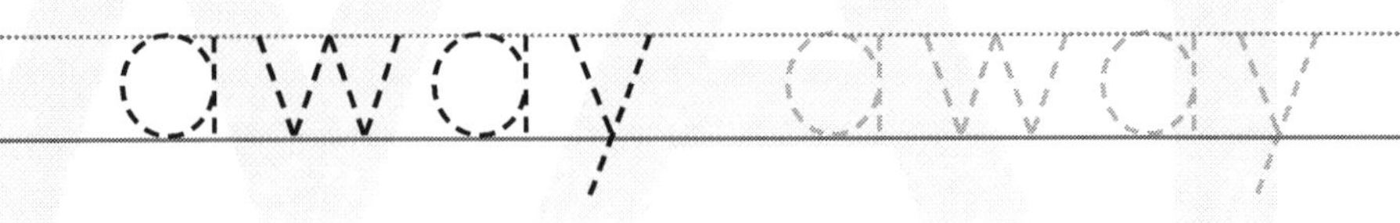

Write the word:

Color the puzzle pieces that have the word "**away**"

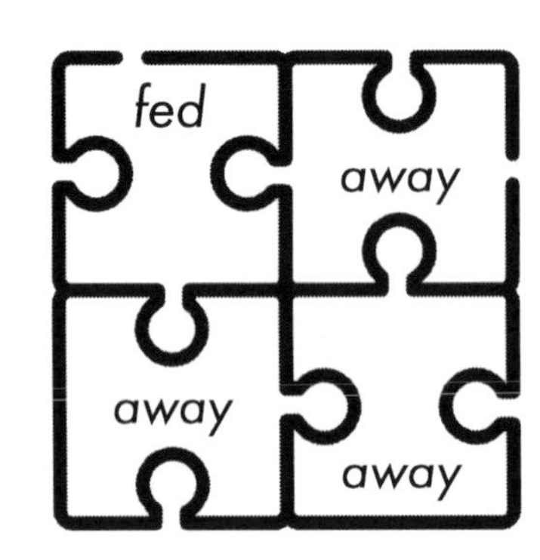

Let's work on our cutting and pasting skills. Cut out the word "**away**" from page 111 and paste it in the square box below to complete the sentence. Then read the sentence aloud!

The bird is flying ______.

Write your own sentence using the word **away**:

This is a **big** house.

Trace the word:

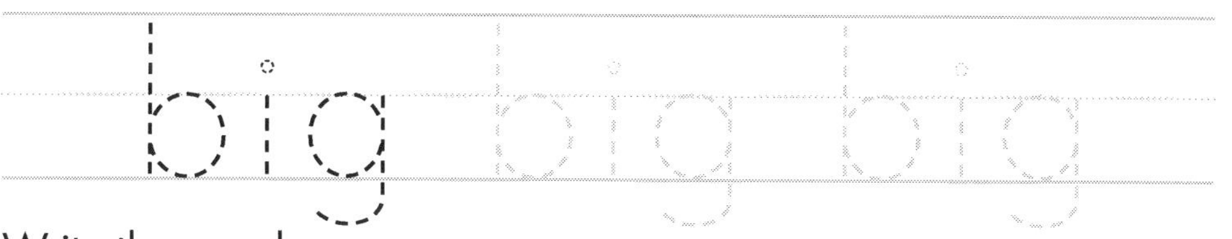

Write the word:

Color the pizza slices that have the word "**big**"

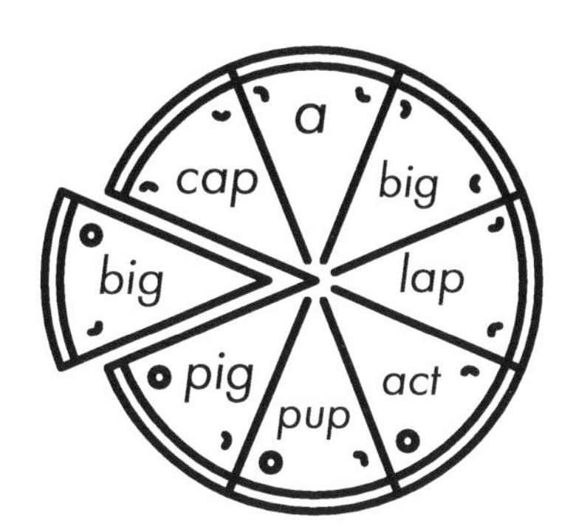

Find and circle the word "**big**"

b	l	j	g	t
k	i	q	l	t
b	i	g	a	b
y	y	z	w	q
v	q	j	f	e

Fill in the missing letters to make the word "**big**"

_ig   b_g

bi_   _ig

bi_   ___

This is a ___ house.

Write your own sentence using the word **big**:

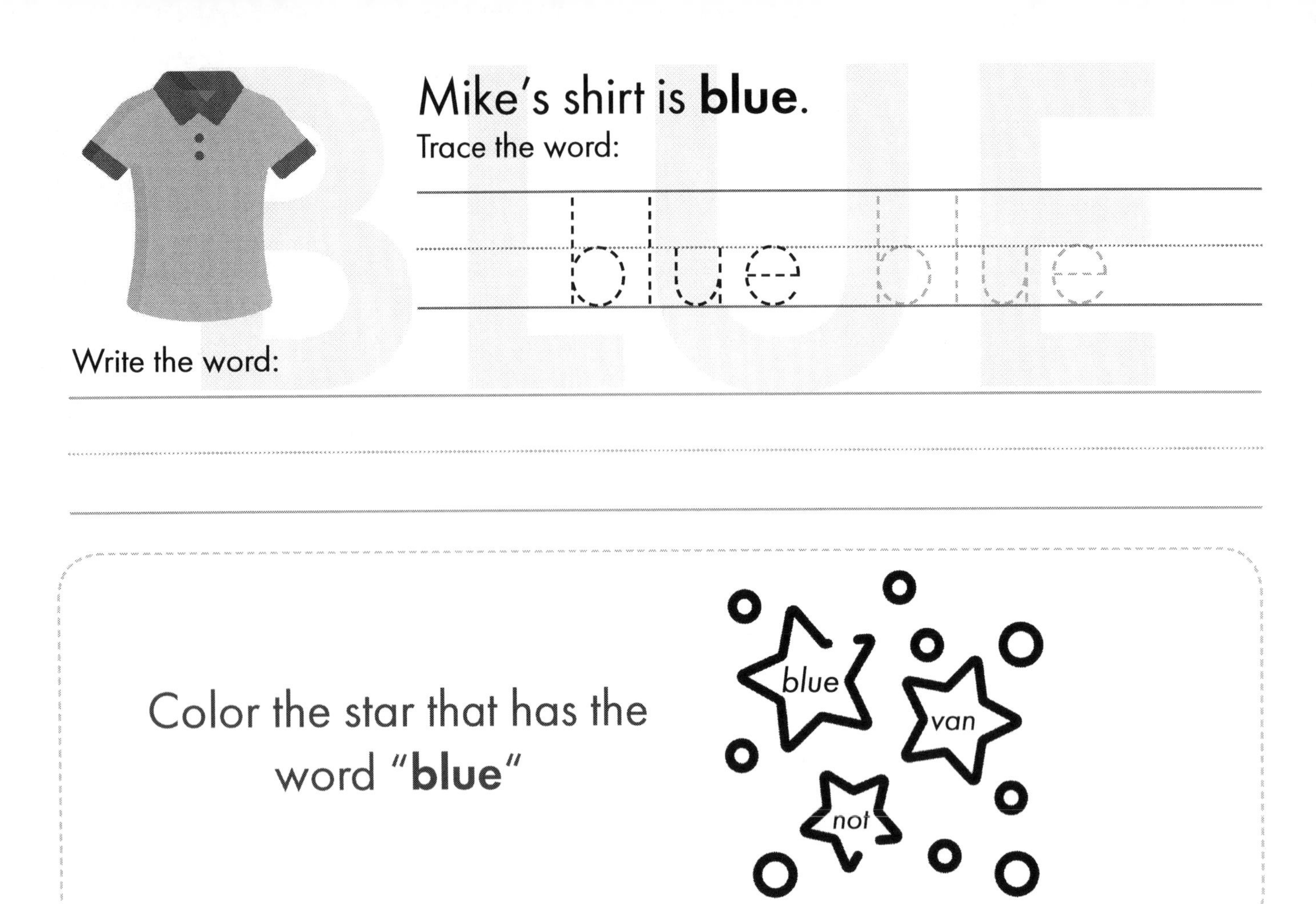

Color the star that has the word "**blue**"

blue
van
not

Let's work on our cutting and pasting skills. Cut out the word "**blue**" from page 111 and paste it in the square box below to complete the sentence. Then read the sentence aloud!

Mike's shirt is ______.

Write your own sentence using the word **blue**:

Can I go to the park?

Trace the word:

Write the word:

Color the pie pieces that have the word "**can**"

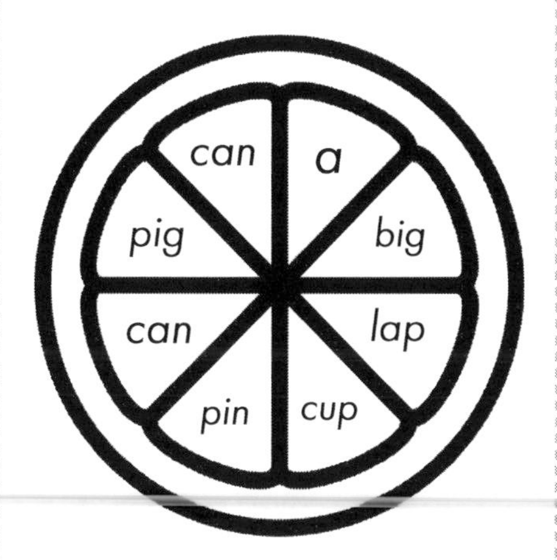

Find and circle the word "**can**"

u	r	s	g	v
u	e	c	x	b
n	a	u	r	w
n	x	k	x	p
a	o	d	r	m

Fill in the missing letters to make the word "**can**"

_an c_n

ca_ _an

ca_ ___

___ I go to the park?

Write your own sentence using the word **can**:

Can Sarah **come** to the park with us?

Trace the word:

come come

Write the word:

Color the pizza slices that have the word "**come**"

Let's work on our cutting and pasting skills. Cut out the word "**come**" from page 111 and paste it in the square box below to complete the sentence. Then read the sentence aloud!

Can Sarah [ ] to the park with us?

Write your own sentence using the word **come**:

Can you write **down** your name?

Trace the word:

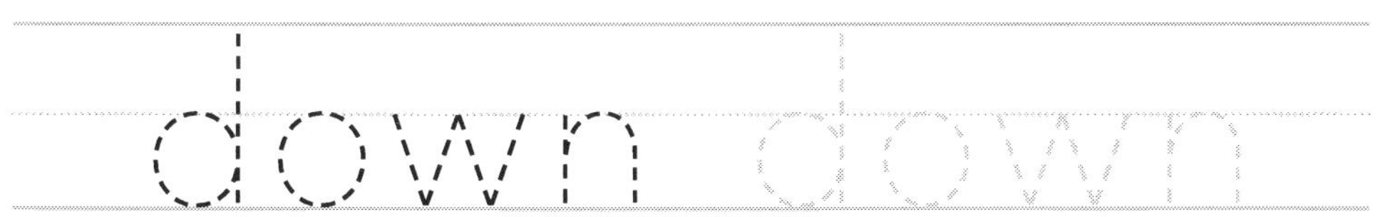

Write the word:

Color the puzzle pieces that have the word "**down**"

Find and circle the word "**down**"

d	v	e	x	j
c	o	d	a	g
d	f	w	k	o
c	u	i	n	t
t	m	t	i	n

Fill in the missing letters to make the word "**down**"

_own d_wn

do__ d_w_

_o_n ____

Can you write ____ your name?

Write your own sentence using the word **down**:

I **need** to find my shoes.

Trace the word:

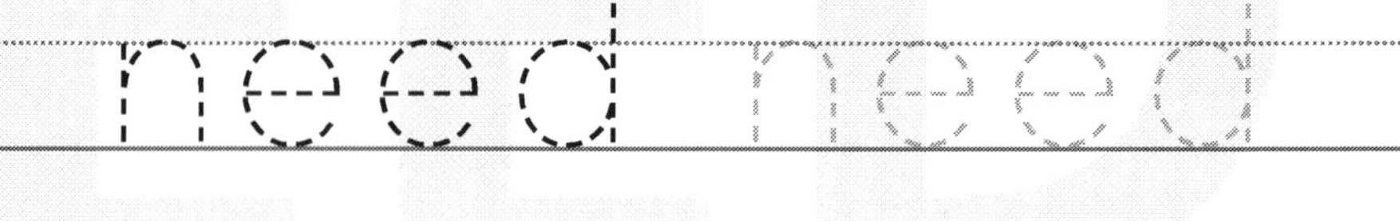

Write the word:

Color the puzzle pieces that have the word "**need**"

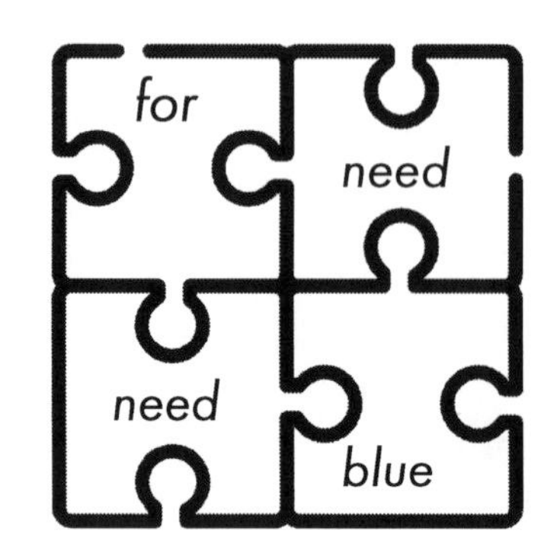

Let's work on our cutting and pasting skills. Cut out the word "**need**" from page 111 and paste it in the square box below to complete the sentence. Then read the sentence aloud!

I [ ] to find my shoes.

Write your own sentence using the word **need**:

This table is too small **for** me.

Trace the word:

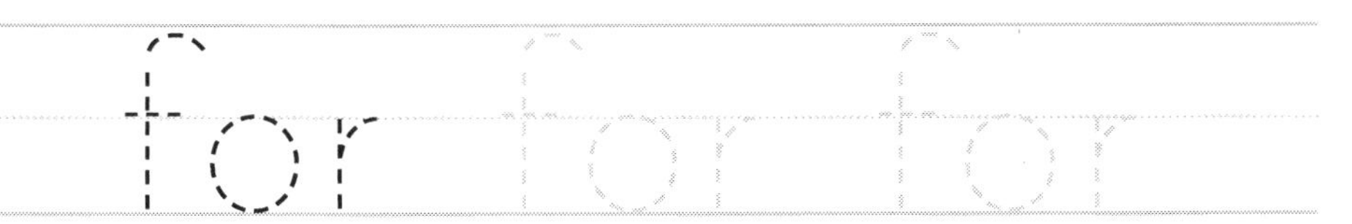

Write the word:

Color the pizza slices that have the word "**for**"

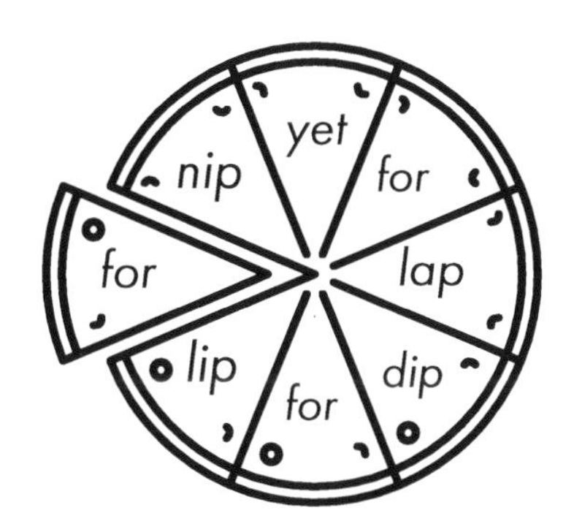

Find and circle the word "**for**"

c	e	v	z	p
c	e	e	t	r
f	o	r	r	c
n	s	o	t	c
p	h	v	k	k

Fill in the missing letters to make the word "**for**"

_or **f_r**

fo_ **_or**

fo_ **___**

This table is too small _ _ _ me.

Write your own sentence using the word **for**:

She is very **funny**!

Trace the word:

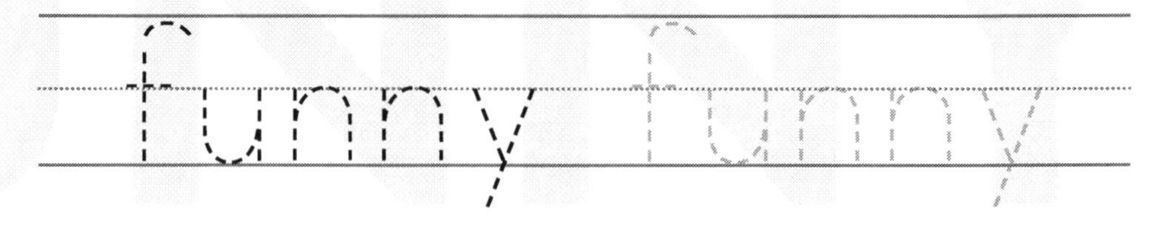

Write the word:

Color the star that has the word "**funny**"

Let's work on our cutting and pasting skills. Cut out the word "**funny**" from page 111 and paste it in the square box below to complete the sentence. Then read the sentence aloud!

She is very [ ] **!**

Write your own sentence using the word **funny**:

We will **go** to the museum.

Trace the word:

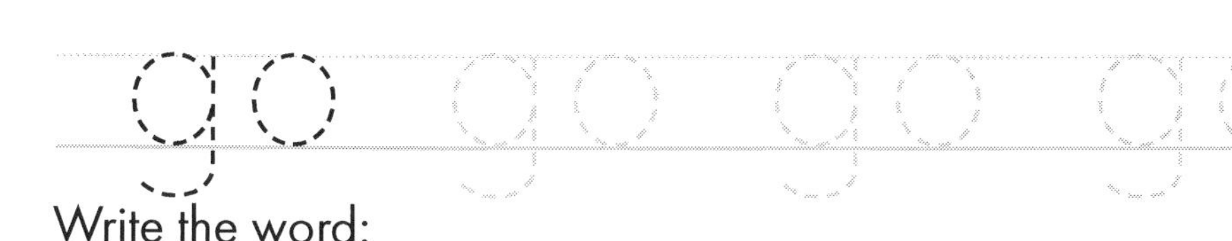

Write the word:

Color the pie pieces that have the word "**go**"

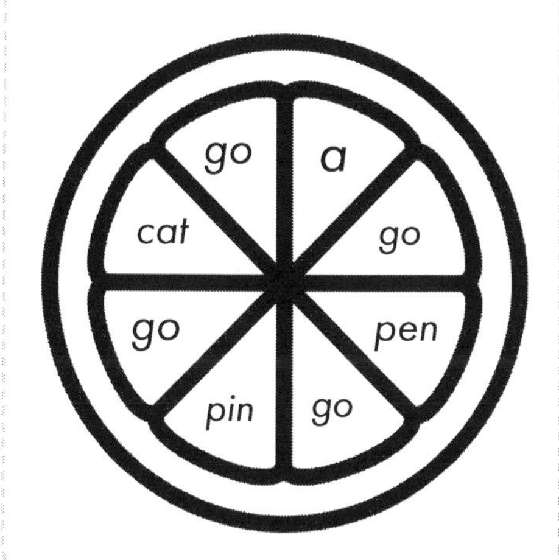

Find and circle the word "**go**"

p j p p i
y t g u s
b f w o x
y c x y s
j n d m n

Fill in the missing letters to make the word "**go**"

_o g_

__ __

g_ _o

We will _ _ to the museum.

Write your own sentence using the word **go**:

I need **help** with my homework.

Trace the word:

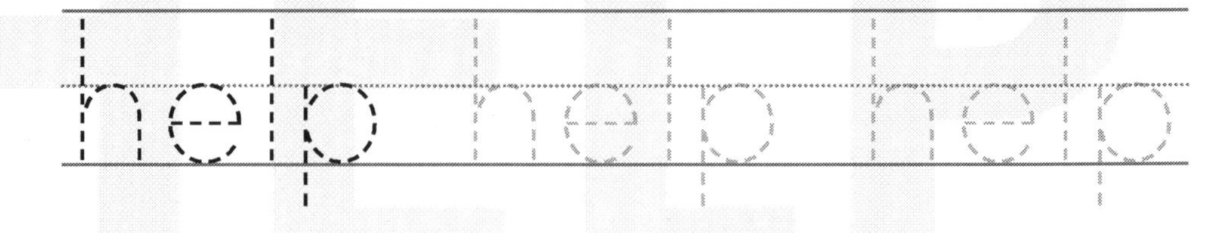

Write the word:

Color the pizza slices that have the word "**help**"

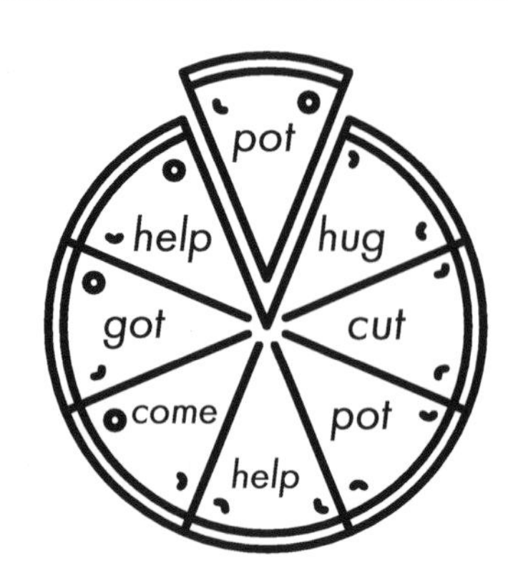

Let's work on our cutting and pasting skills. Cut out the word "**help**" from page 111 and paste it in the square box below to complete the sentence. Then read the sentence aloud!

I need [ ] with my homework.

Write your own sentence using the word **help**:

Tom will be **here** any minute.

Trace the word:

here here here

Write the word:

Color the puzzle pieces that have the word "**here**"

Find and circle the word "**here**"

t	e	t	e	q
t	u	r	i	y
t	e	d	o	u
h	d	p	q	m
s	i	k	l	y

Fill in the missing letters to make the word "**here**"

_ere **h_ere**

he__ **h_r_**

_e_e **____**

Tom will be _ _ _ _ any minute.

Write your own sentence using the word **here**:

I want to be an astronaut.

Trace the word:

I I I I I

Write the word:

Color the puzzle pieces that have the word "**I**"

Let's work on our cutting and pasting skills. Cut out the word "**I**" from page 111 and paste it in the square box below to complete the sentence. Then read the sentence aloud!

[ ] want to be an astronaut.

Write your own sentence using the word **I**:

I live **in** New York City.

Trace the word:

in in in in in

Write the word:

Color the pizza slices that have the word "**in**"

Find and circle the word "**in**"

o g e x x
i n x z f
h e r t c
r v q s m
r m d m e

Fill in the missing letters to make the word "**in**"

_n i_ __
i_ _n __
__ __ __

I live _ _ New York City.

Write your own sentence using the word **in**:

My mom **is** the best!

Trace the word:

is is is is is

Write the word:

Color the star that has the word "**is**"

Let's work on our cutting and pasting skills. Cut out the word "**is**" from page 111 and paste it in the square box below to complete the sentence. Then read the sentence aloud!

My mom [ ] the best!

Write your own sentence using the word **is**:

It is hot today.

Trace the word:

It It It It It

Write the word:

Color the pie pieces that have the word "**It**"

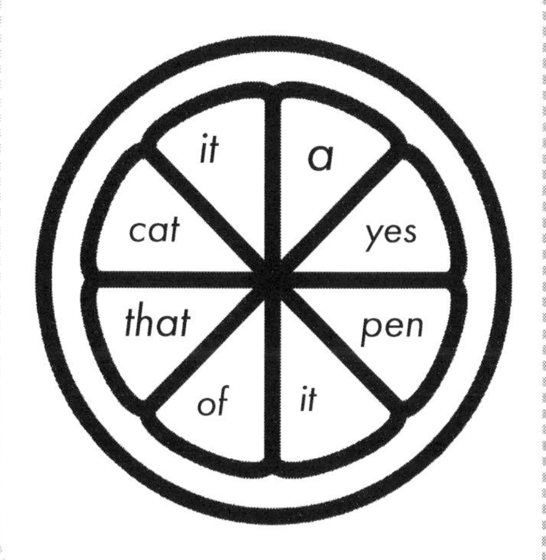

Find and circle the word "**It**"

p	j	p	p	i
y	t	r	u	s
b	f	w	o	x
y	c	x	y	s
j	n	d	m	n

Fill in the missing letters to make the word "**It**"

_t I_ __

I_ _t __

__ __ __

_ _ is hot today.

Write your own sentence using the word **it**:

Can I **jump** in the pool?

Trace the word:

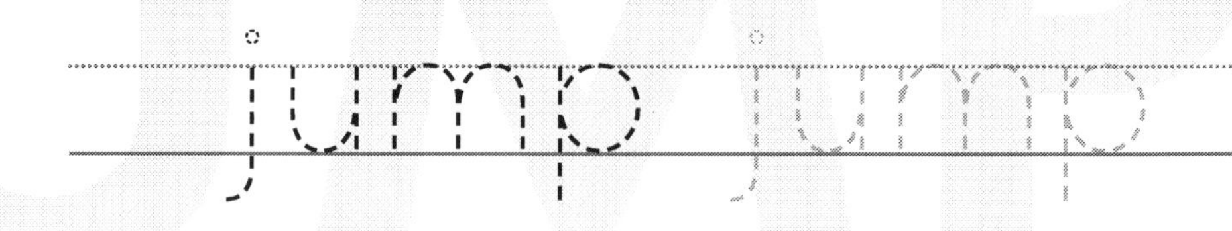

Write the word:

Color the pizza slices that have the word "**jump**"

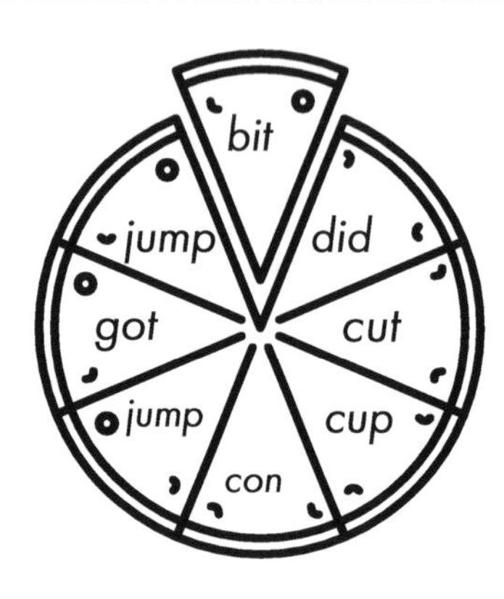

Let's work on our cutting and pasting skills. Cut out the word "**jump**" from page 111 and paste it in the square box below to complete the sentence. Then read the sentence aloud!

Can I [ ] in the pool?

Write your own sentence using the word **jump**:

It is a **little** cold today.

Trace the word:

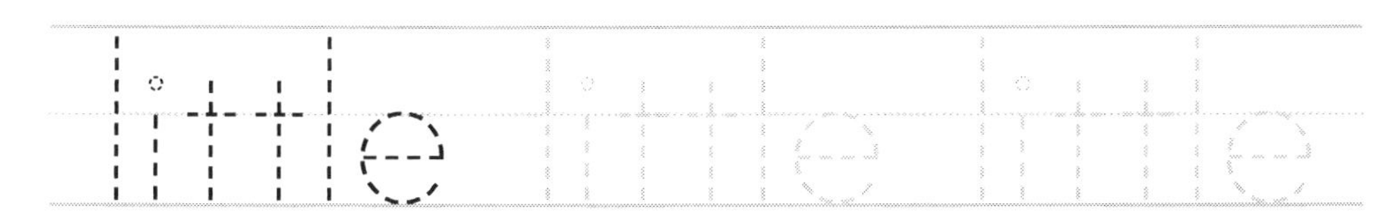

Write the word:

Color the puzzle pieces that have the word "**little**"

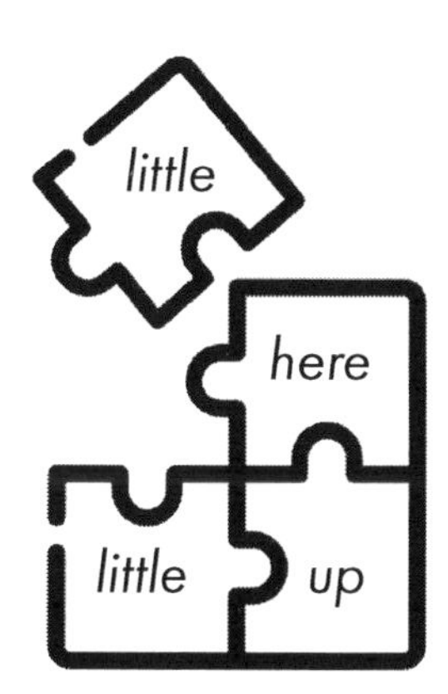

Find and circle the word "**little**"

v	v	g	a	b	l
r	o	u	x	i	s
q	d	n	t	k	n
w	d	t	g	w	h
s	l	g	d	b	c
e	e	h	e	d	g

Fill in the missing letters to make the word "**little**"

_ittle l_ttle

l_t_l_e litt__

__tt__ ______

It is a ______ cold today.

Write your own sentence using the word **little**:

Look at the beautiful mountain!

Trace the word:

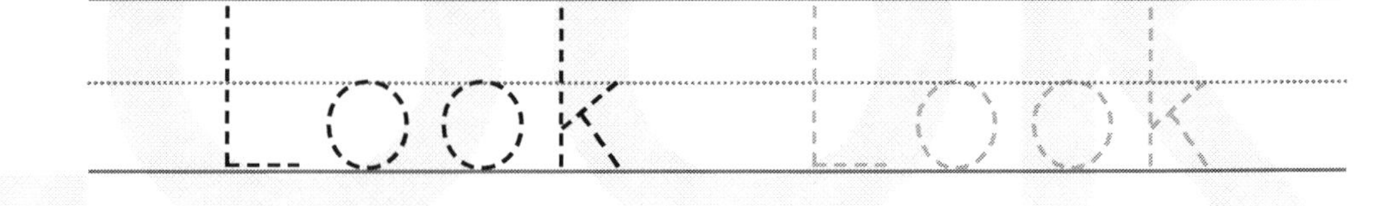

Write the word:

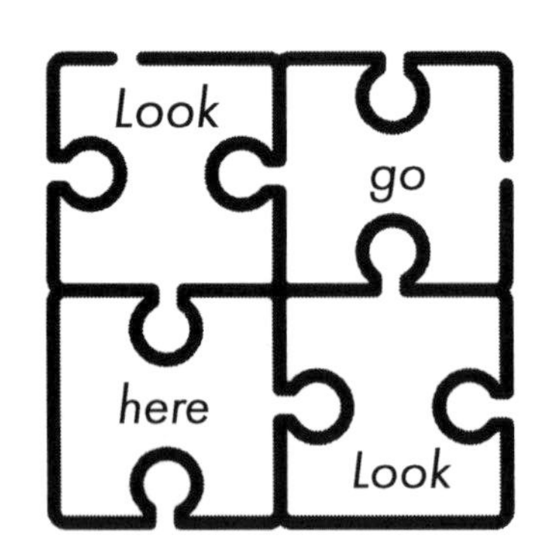

Color the puzzle pieces that have the word "**Look**"

Let's work on our cutting and pasting skills. Cut out the word "**Look**" from page 111 and paste it in the square box below to complete the sentence. Then read the sentence aloud!

at the beautiful mountain!

Write your own sentence using the word **look**:

Can I **make** a cake?

Trace the word:

make make

Write the word:

Color the pizza slices that have the word "**make**"

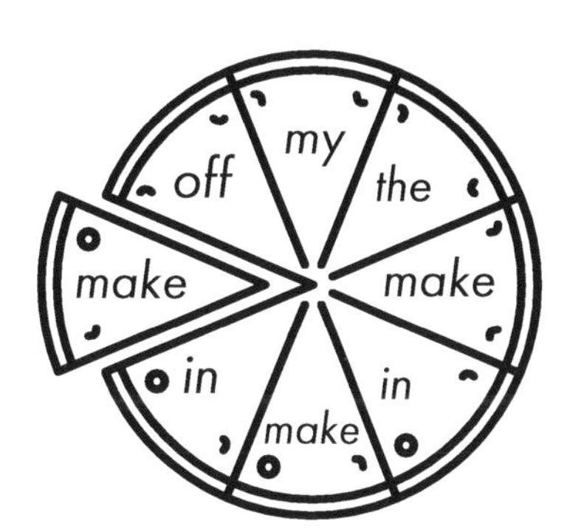

Find and circle the word "**make**"

d	e	v	s	y
m	a	k	e	g
g	t	c	e	q
l	x	n	p	x
r	a	e	e	h

Fill in the missing letters to make the word "**make**"

_ake   m_ke

ma__   m_k_

_a_e   ____

Can I _ _ _ _ a cake?

Write your own sentence using the word **make**:

My parents love **me**.

Trace the word:

me me me me

Write the word:

Color the stars that have the word "**me**"

Let's work on our cutting and pasting skills. Cut out the word "**me**" from page 111 and paste it in the square box below to complete the sentence. Then read the sentence aloud!

My parents love [ ].

Write your own sentence using the word **me**:

My teacher is smart.

Trace the word:

My My my my

Write the word:

Color the pie pieces that have the word "**My**"

Find and circle the word "**My**"

f w g d t j
q m d d y h
y h c v l q
r x h h n c
r i e f l a
f t b v b w

Fill in the missing letters to make the word "**My**"

_y m_ __
m_ _y __
__ __ __

_ _ teacher is smart.

Write your own sentence using the word **my**:

The door does **not** open.

Trace the word:

not not not

Write the word:

Color the pizza slices that have the word "**not**"

Let's work on our cutting and pasting skills. Cut out the word "**not**" from page 111 and paste it in the square box below to complete the sentence. Then read the sentence aloud!

The door does ☐ open.

Write your own sentence using the word **not**:

I have **one** brother.

Trace the word:

Write the word:

Color the puzzle pieces that have the word "**one**"

Find and circle the word "**one**"

p	r	r	a	o	f
k	e	s	t	n	h
h	j	c	m	e	c
y	l	k	a	s	e
k	h	x	n	z	h
d	s	w	g	p	h

Fill in the missing letters to make the word "**one**"

_ne   o_e   __e

_n_   ___   on_

___   ___   ___

I have _ _ _ brother.

Write your own sentence using the word **one**:

I can **play** the guitar.

Trace the word:

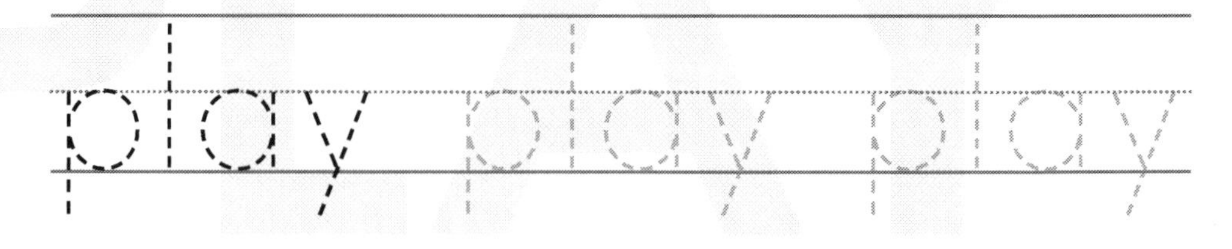

Write the word:

Color the puzzle pieces that have the word "**play**"

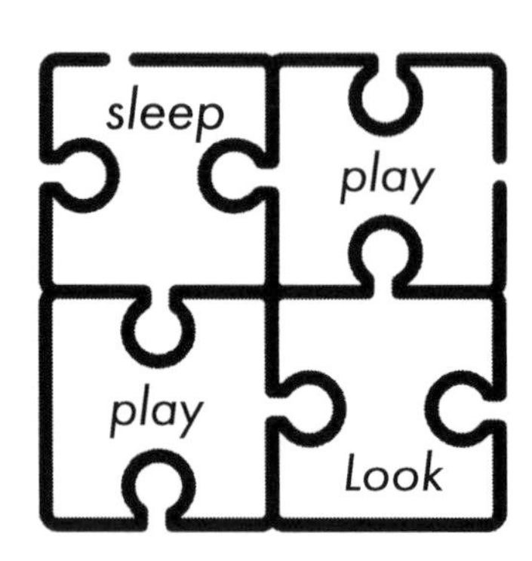

Let's work on our cutting and pasting skills. Cut out the word "**play**" from page 111 and paste it in the square box below to complete the sentence. Then read the sentence aloud!

I can [ ] the guitar.

Write your own sentence using the word **play**:

My favorite color is **red**.

Trace the word:

Write the word:

Color the pizza slices that have the word "**red**"	Find and circle the word "**red**"	Fill in the missing letters to make the word "**red**"
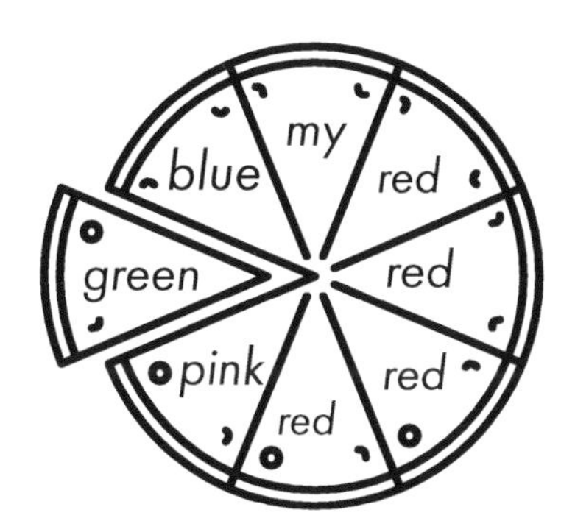	f d u c t w k e o p t v i r l d g q a c n s h b i k d w i k f r z h g p	**_ed r_d __d** **re_ __d ___** **r__ _e_ ___**

My favorite color is _ _ _.

Write your own sentence using the word **red**:

She can **run** very fast.

Trace the word:

run run run run

Write the word:

Color the star that has the word "**run**"

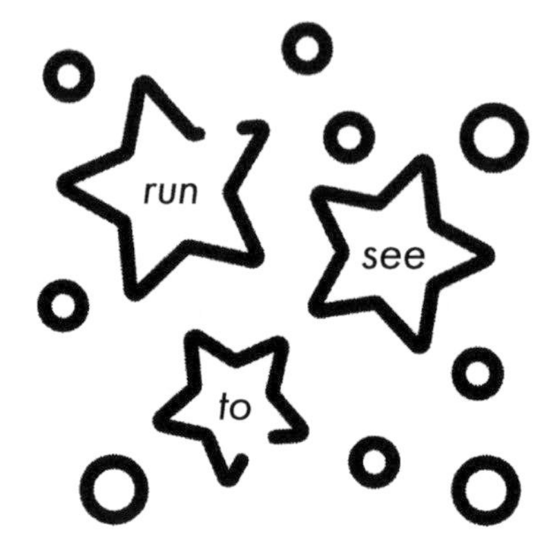

Let's work on our cutting and pasting skills. Cut out the word "**run**" from page 111 and paste it in the square box below to complete the sentence. Then read the sentence aloud!

She can [ ] very fast.

Write your own sentence using the word **run**:

She **said** goodbye.

Trace the word:

said said said

Write the word:

Color the pie pieces that have the word "**said**"

Find and circle the word "**said**"

p l k j l x
k m x j q y
c d i a s d
r f r s f a
y v i j z s
v z j j t o

Fill in the missing letters to make the word "**said**"

_aid sa__

__id s_i_

_a_d ____

She _ _ _ _ goodbye.

Write your own sentence using the word **said**:

I **see** a car.

Trace the word:

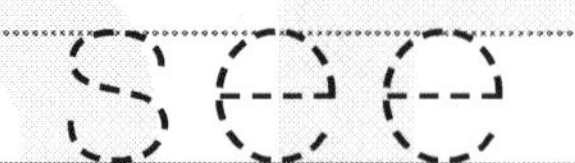

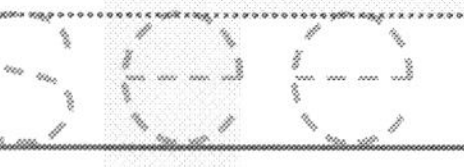

Write the word:

Color the pizza slices that have the word "**see**"

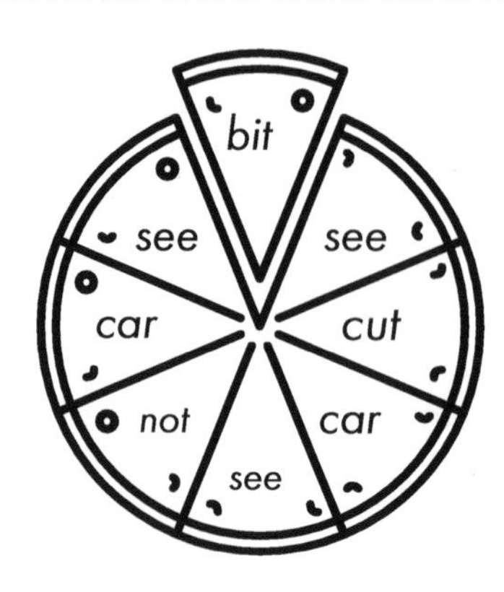

Let's work on our cutting and pasting skills. Cut out the word "**see**" from page 111 and paste it in the square box below to complete the sentence. Then read the sentence aloud!

Write your own sentence using the word **see**:

The light is bright.

Trace the word:

The The The

Write the word:

Color the puzzle pieces that have the word "**The**"

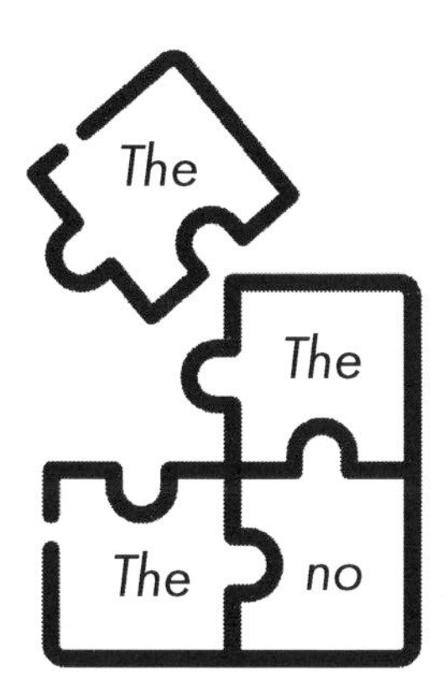

Find and circle the word "**The**"

z e y n g p
g h b k f u
p t l k m b
w w a s g y
k g t g g k
p d p m c r

Fill in the missing letters to make the word "**The**"

_he T_e __e

_h_ ___ Th_

___ ___ ___

___ light is bright.

Write your own sentence using the word **the**:

I have **three** siblings.

Trace the word:

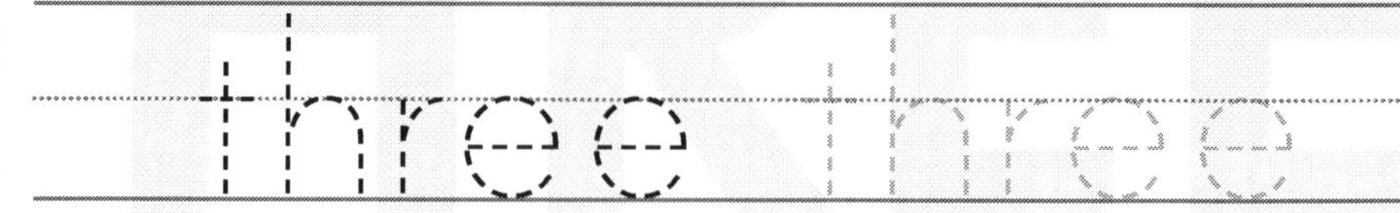

Write the word:

Color the puzzle pieces that have the word "**three**"

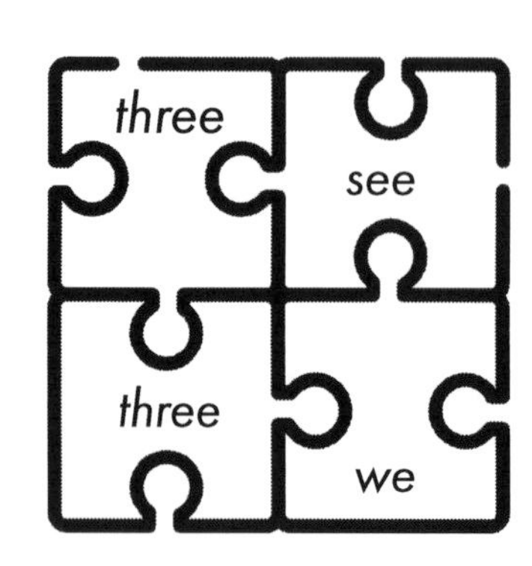

Let's work on our cutting and pasting skills. Cut out the word "**three**" from page 111 and paste it in the square box below to complete the sentence. Then read the sentence aloud!

I have [ ] siblings.

Write your own sentence using the word **three**:

Kate likes **to** study.

Trace the word:

Write the word:

Color the pizza slices that have the word "**to**"

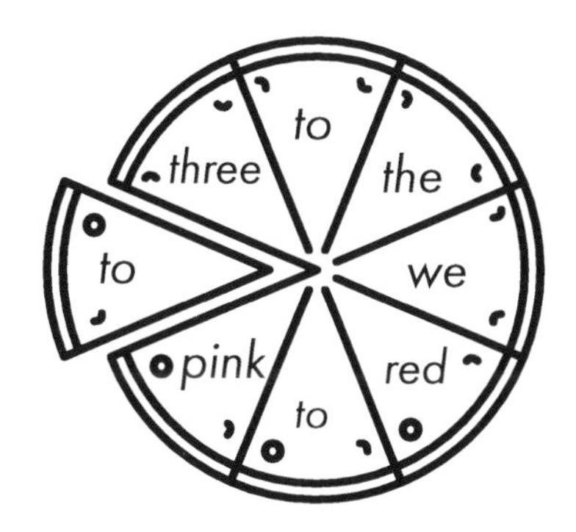

Find and circle the word "**to**"

o z k j h d
t m x s g e
k u b y s c
b g g q n c
j l m e q m
h c s w q y

Fill in the missing letters to make the word "**to**"

_o t_ __
__ _o t_
__ __ __

Kate likes _ _ study.

Write your own sentence using the word **to**:

There are **two** plants.

Trace the word:

Write the word:

Color the star that has the word "**two**"

Let's work on our cutting and pasting skills. Cut out the word "**two**" from page 111 and paste it in the square box below to complete the sentence. Then read the sentence aloud!

There are [ ] plants.

Write your own sentence using the word **two**:

The sun is **up**.

Trace the word:

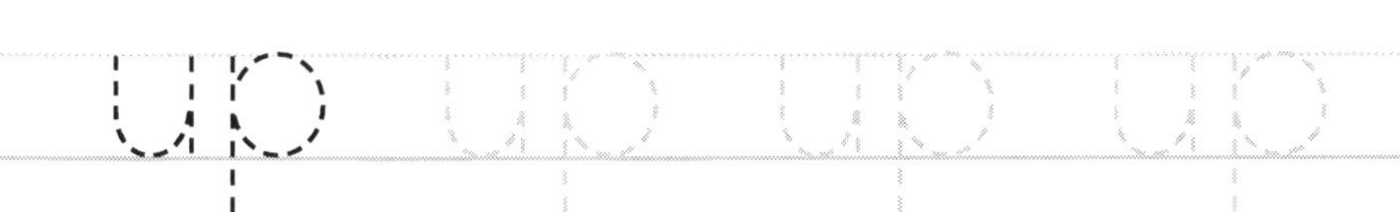

Write the word:

Color the pie pieces that have the word "**up**"

Find and circle the word "**up**"

g u g u x d
p b r o o z
r e w k n x
l v e d f i
m d v d l i
b w c g x s

Fill in the missing letters to make the word "**up**"

_p u_ __
__ _p u_
__ __ __

The sun is _ _.

Write your own sentence using the word **up**:

We are happy.

Trace the word:

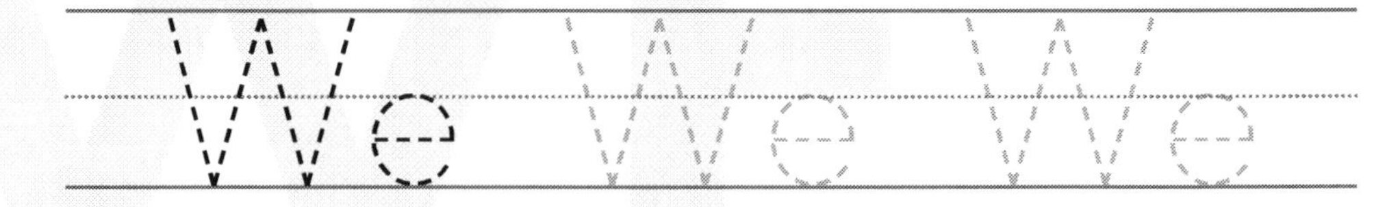

Write the word:

Color the pizza slices that have the word "**we**"

Let's work on our cutting and pasting skills. Cut out the word "**We**" from page 111 and paste it in the square box below to complete the sentence. Then read the sentence aloud!

Write your own sentence using the word **we**:

Where are you from?

Trace the word:

Write the word:

Color the puzzle pieces that have the word "**Where**"

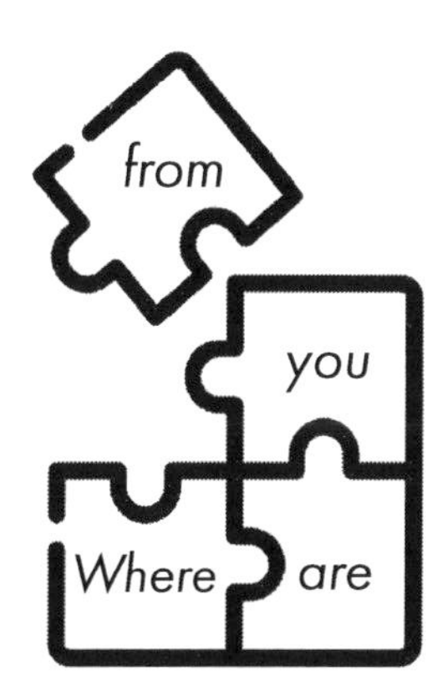

Find and circle the word "**Where**"

e	f	b	k	b	h
u	r	n	u	f	z
n	k	e	p	f	v
v	p	s	h	a	j
a	o	f	p	w	z
c	w	k	o	n	l

Fill in the missing letters to make the word "**Where**"

_here **W_e_e**

___re **_h_r_**

_____ **____e**

_____ are you from?

Write your own sentence using the word **where**:

The banana is **yellow**.

Trace the word:

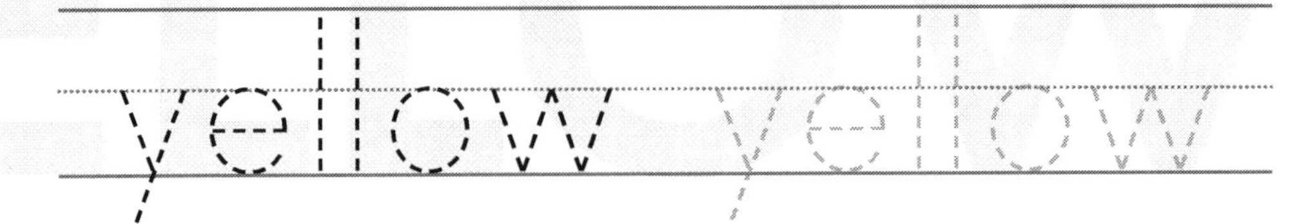

Write the word:

Color the puzzle pieces that have the word "**yellow**"

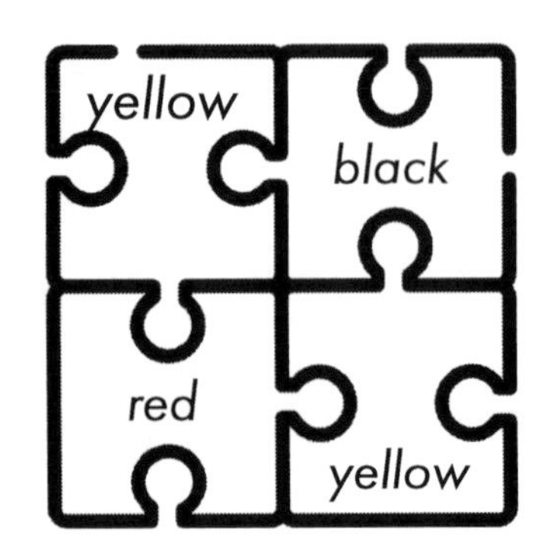

Let's work on our cutting and pasting skills. Cut out the word "**yellow**" from page 111 and paste it in the square box below to complete the sentence. Then read the sentence aloud!

The banana is [ ] .

Write your own sentence using the word **yellow**:

You look tired.

Trace the word:

You You You

Write the word:

Color the pizza slices that have the word "**You**"

Find and circle the word "**You**"

m	j	k	j	w	u
u	k	d	z	i	u
u	i	m	s	o	k
s	c	s	y	u	h
m	y	l	m	p	o
y	k	z	l	p	v

Fill in the missing letters to make the word "**You**"

_ou Y_u __u

_o_ ___ Yo_

___ ___ ___

___ look tired.

Write your own sentence using the word **you**:

We are **all** family.

Trace the word:

all all all all

Write the word:

Color the stars that have the word "**all**"

Let's work on our cutting and pasting skills. Cut out the word "**all**" from page 111 and paste it in the square box below to complete the sentence. Then read the sentence aloud!

We are [ ] family.

Write your own sentence using the word **all**:

I **am** hungry.

Trace the word:

am am am am

Write the word:

Color the pie pieces that have the word "**am**"

Find and circle the word "**am**"

k g p w e h
p p a m i u
q a s z i h
c j t p q z
t i l n h k
p f w a z v

Fill in the missing letters to make the word "**am**"

_m **a_** **__**

__ **_m** **a_**

__ **__** **__**

I _ _ hungry.

Write your own sentence using the word **am**:

How **are** you?

Trace the word:

are are are

Write the word:

Color the pizza slices that have the word "**are**"

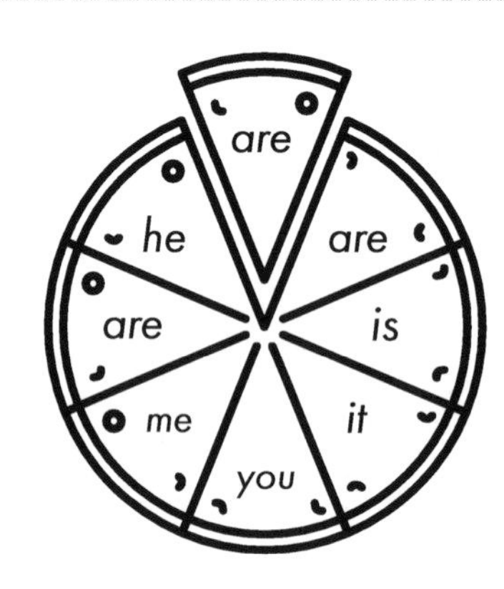

Let's work on our cutting and pasting skills. Cut out the word "**are**" from page 111 and paste it in the square box below to complete the sentence. Then read the sentence aloud!

Write your own sentence using the word **are**:

I am **at** school.

Trace the word:

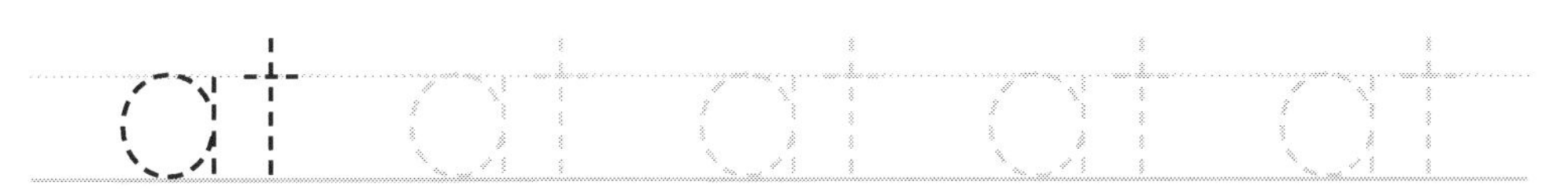

Write the word:

Color the puzzle pieces that have the word "**at**"	Find and circle the word "**at**"	Fill in the missing letters to make the word "**at**"
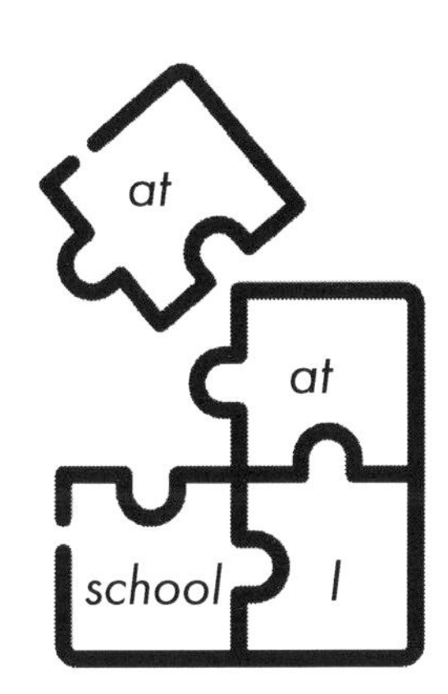	d i i u l v r a y s f k c b t b y i y b e c q g g l d f a i a n o x d a	_t a_ __ __ _t a_ __ __ __

I am _ _ school.

Write your own sentence using the word **at**:

We **ate** some apples.

Trace the word:

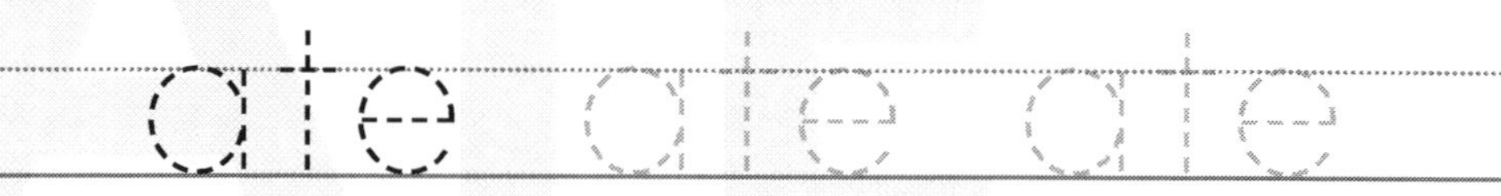

Write the word:

Color the puzzle pieces that have the word "**ate**"

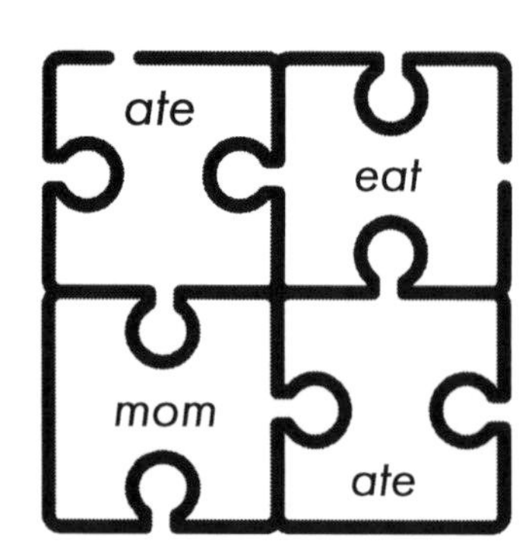

Let's work on our cutting and pasting skills. Cut out the word "**ate**" from page 111 and paste it in the square box below to complete the sentence. Then read the sentence aloud!

We [ ] some apples.

Write your own sentence using the word **ate**:

I will **be** right back.

Trace the word:

Write the word:

Color the pizza slices that have the word "**be**"

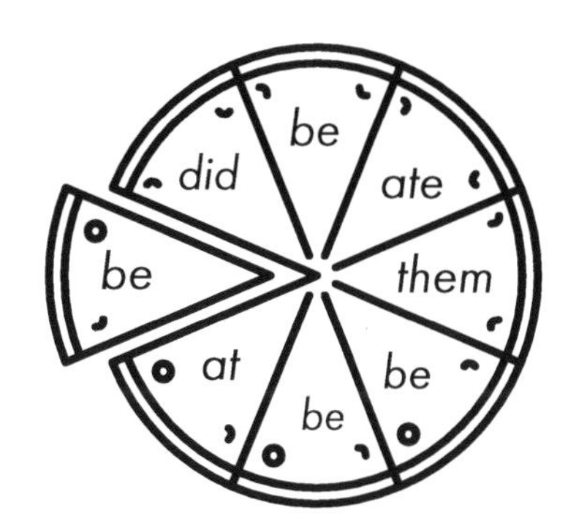

Find and circle the word "**be**"

j	m	t	l	l	i
h	x	g	n	x	s
z	a	u	e	k	o
t	v	b	e	u	e
z	r	o	i	m	q
k	z	f	m	a	x

Fill in the missing letters to make the word "**be**"

_e **b_** **__**

__ **_e** **b_**

__ __ __

I will _ _ right back.

Write your own sentence using the word **be**:

He has **black** shoes.

Trace the word:

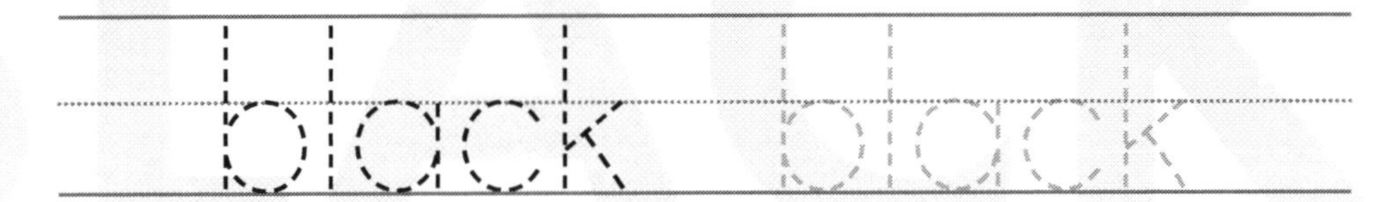

Write the word:

Color the star that has the word "**black**"

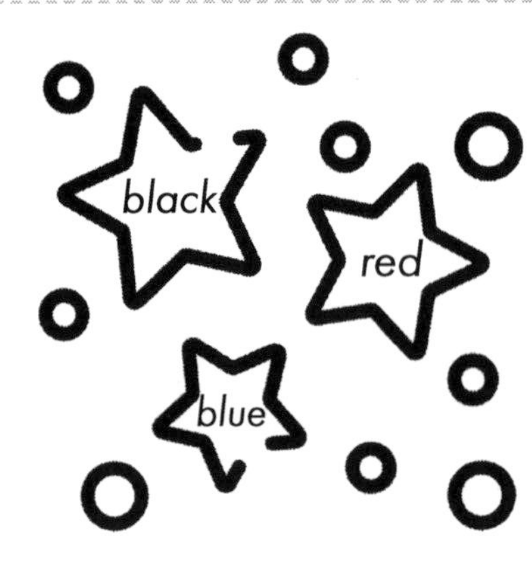

Let's work on our cutting and pasting skills. Cut out the word "**black**" from page 111 and paste it in the square box below to complete the sentence. Then read the sentence aloud!

He has [ ] shoes.

Write your own sentence using the word **black**:

The rug is **brown**.

Trace the word:

brown brown

Write the word:

Color the pie pieces that have the word "**brown**"

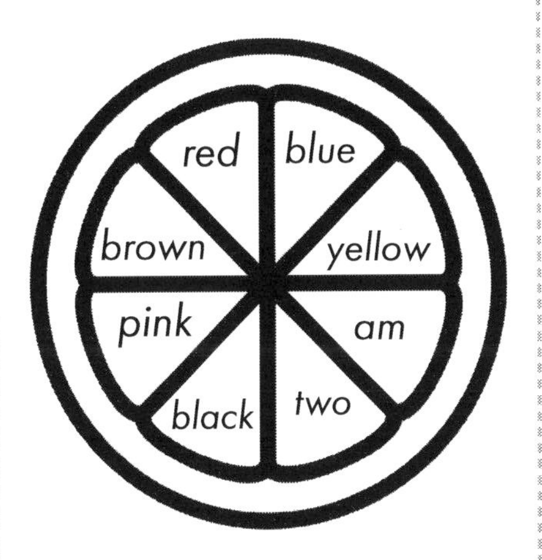

Find and circle the word "**brown**"

l	r	x	r	s	o
j	g	l	f	f	v
t	p	k	g	o	f
q	j	w	k	b	p
e	n	w	o	r	b
x	k	l	g	v	h

Fill in the missing letters to make the word "**brown**"

_rown **b_o_n**

___wn **_r_w_**

_____ **____n**

The rug is _____.

Write your own sentence using the word **brown**:

I want to play in the park **but** it's raining.

Trace the word:

but but but

Write the word:

Color the pizza slices that have the word "**but**"

Let's work on our cutting and pasting skills. Cut out the word "**but**" from page 113 and paste it in the square box below to complete the sentence. Then read the sentence aloud!

I want to play in the park [ ] it's raining.

Write your own sentence using the word **but**:

My friend **came** over to my house.

Trace the word:

came came

Write the word:

Color the puzzle pieces that have the word "**came**"

Find and circle the word "**came**"

b	c	x	x	d	j
y	l	o	b	d	g
e	m	a	c	f	d
y	y	z	p	r	s
e	y	c	g	k	x
j	f	p	k	c	s

Fill in the missing letters to make the word "**came**"

_ame **c_m_**

__me **_a_e**

____ **___e**

My friend ____ over to my house.

Write your own sentence using the word **came**:

Did you finish your homework?

Trace the word:

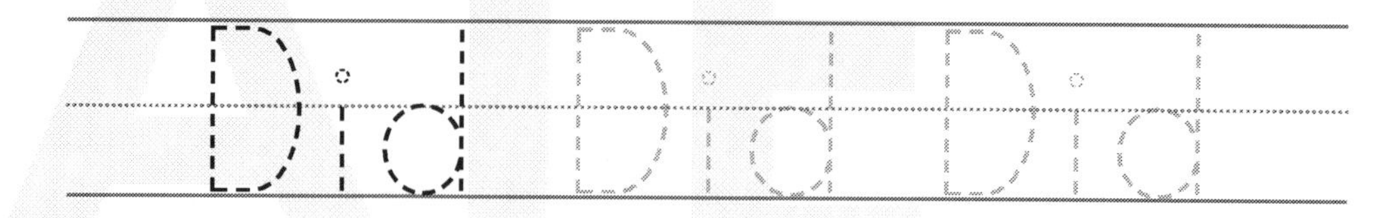

Write the word:

Color the puzzle pieces that have the word "**Did**"

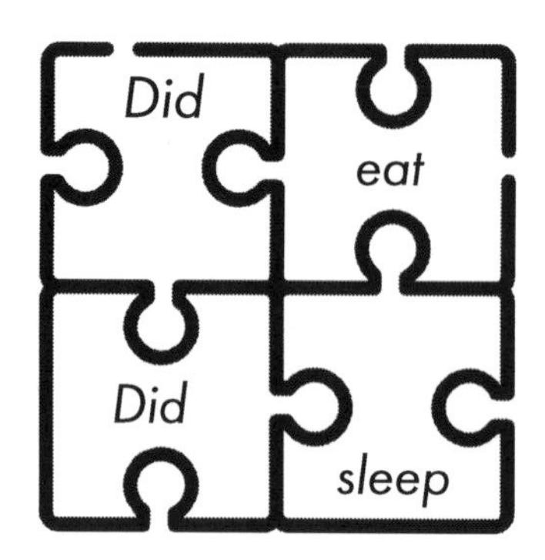

Let's work on our cutting and pasting skills. Cut out the word "**Did**" from page 113 and paste it in the square box below to complete the sentence. Then read the sentence aloud!

[ ] you finish your homework?

Write your own sentence using the word **did**:

Do you know how to bake?

Trace the word:

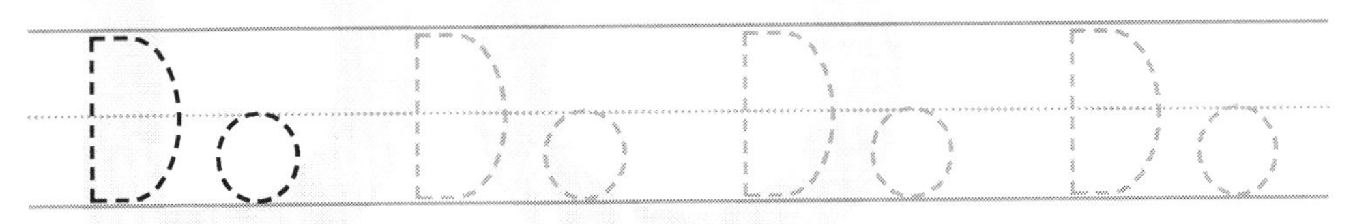

Write the word:

Color the pizza slices that have the word "**Do**"

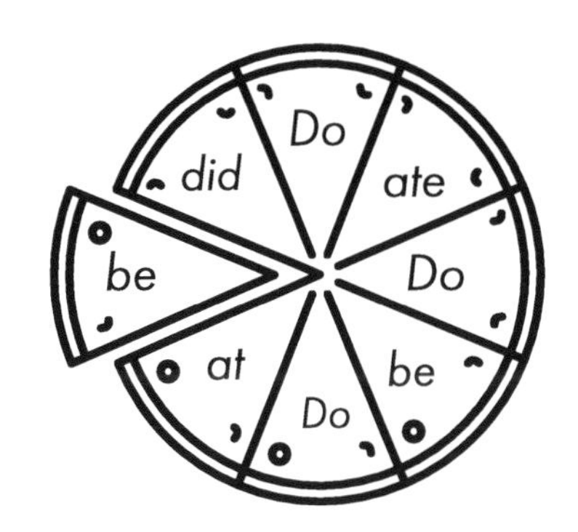

Find and circle the word "**Do**"

k w n t a d
x h m r v i
h n d r v j
x y o f s x
s v r o f e
m c z x g f

Fill in the missing letters to make the word "**Do**"

_o D_ __
__ _o D_
__ __ __

__ you know how to bake?

Write your own sentence using the word **do**:

I like to **eat** carrots.

Trace the word:

eat eat eat

Write the word:

Color the star that has the word "**eat**"

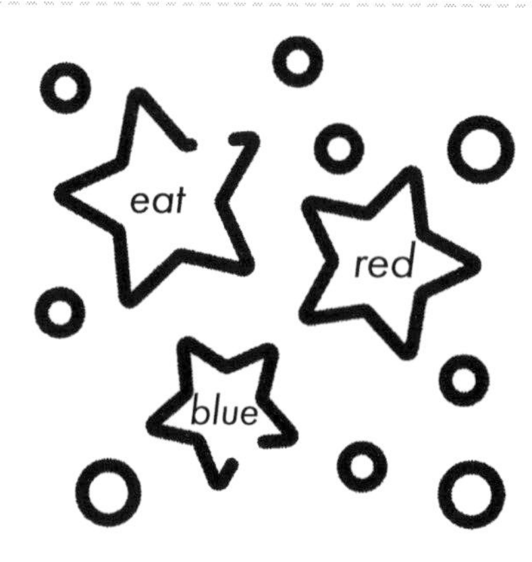

Let's work on our cutting and pasting skills. Cut out the word "**eat**" from page 113 and paste it in the square box below to complete the sentence. Then read the sentence aloud!

I like to [ ] carrots.

Write your own sentence using the word **eat**:

My sister is **four** years old.

Trace the word:

four four four

Write the word:

Color the pie pieces that have the word "**four**"

Find and circle the word "**four**"

t q f g d d
k k x o u e
f f t v u y
z u c j l r
i t u j n k
e c r f a z

Fill in the missing letters to make the word "**four**"

_our f_u_

__ur _o_r

____ ___r

My sister is _ _ _ _ years old.

Write your own sentence using the word **four**:

I usually **get** up at eight.

Trace the word:

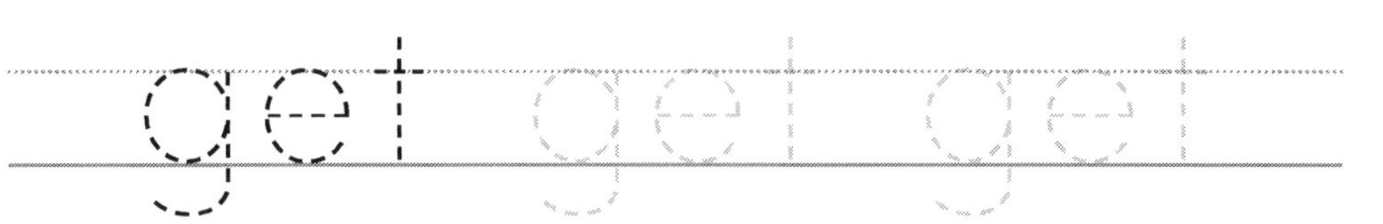

Write the word:

Color the pizza slices that have the word "**get**"

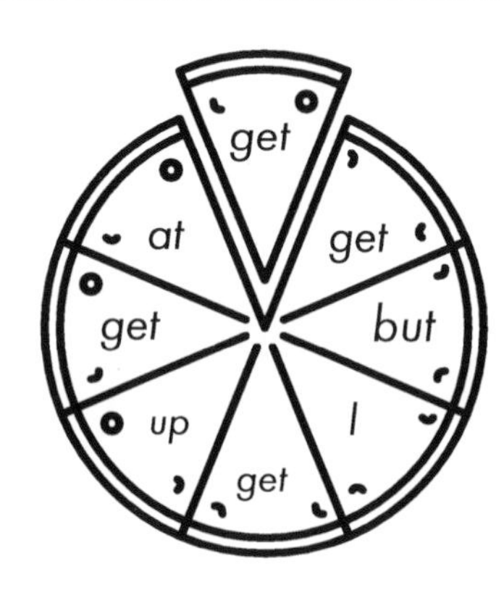

Let's work on our cutting and pasting skills. Cut out the word "**get**" from page 113 and paste it in the square box below to complete the sentence. Then read the sentence aloud!

I usually [ ] up at eight.

Write your own sentence using the word **get**:

This tastes **good**!

Trace the word:

good good

Write the word:

Color the puzzle pieces that have the word "**good**"

Find and circle the word "**good**"

p	d	j	e	t	n
t	o	e	c	z	n
n	f	g	b	c	x
k	y	i	o	q	b
s	f	s	t	o	v
h	h	u	x	w	d

Fill in the missing letters to make the word "**good**"

_ood   **g_o_**

__od   **_o_d**

____   **___d**

This tastes _ _ _ _!

Write your own sentence using the word **good**:

Do you **have** a dog?

Trace the word:

have have

Write the word:

Color the puzzle pieces that have the word "**have**"

Let's work on our cutting and pasting skills. Cut out the word "**have**" from page 113 and paste it in the square box below to complete the sentence. Then read the sentence aloud!

Do you [ ] a dog?

Write your own sentence using the word **have**:

He is very smart.

Trace the word:

he he he he

Write the word:

Color the pizza slices that have the word "**He**"

Find and circle the word "**He**"

y	o	d	u	u	c
n	h	u	f	a	d
d	l	e	n	x	o
k	d	h	e	x	e
v	k	m	o	j	f
j	l	n	m	m	j

Fill in the missing letters to make the word "**He**"

_e **H_** **__**

__ **_e** **H_**

__ **__** **__**

_ _ is very smart.

Write your own sentence using the word **He**:

I put my pants **into** the washing machine.

Trace the word:

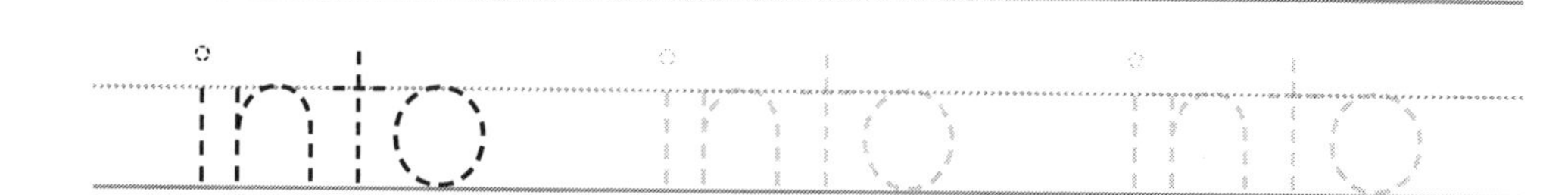

Write the word:

Color the stars that have the word "**into**"

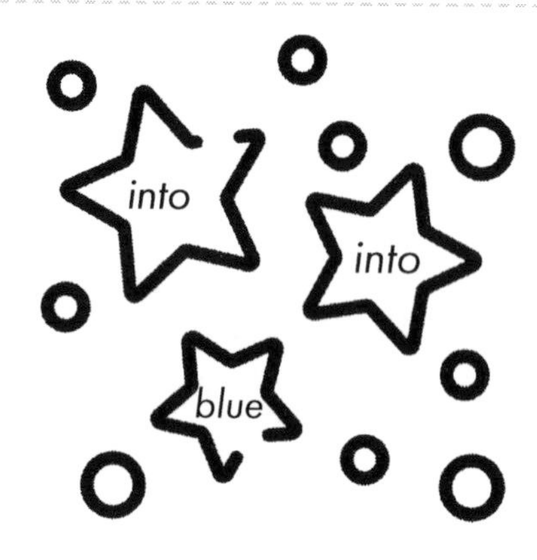

Let's work on our cutting and pasting skills. Cut out the word "**into**" from page 113 and paste it in the square box below to complete the sentence. Then read the sentence aloud!

I put my pants [ ] the washing machine.

Write your own sentence using the word **into**:

I **like** to dance.

Trace the word:

like like like

Write the word:

Color the pie pieces that have the word "**like**"	Find and circle the word "**like**"	Fill in the missing letters to make the word "**like**"
	g e u i d i e k i l f p c r t m e j a x h c y a n v s a y q f a p v o p	_ike l_k_ __ke _ik_ ____ ___e

I _ _ _ _ to dance.

Write your own sentence using the word **like**:

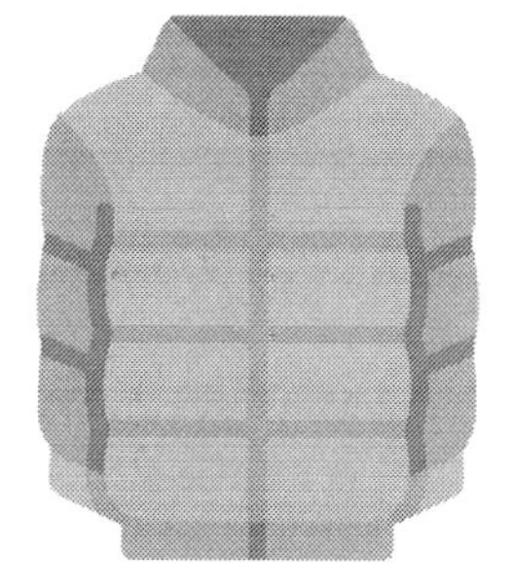

You **must** wear a jacket in the winter.

Trace the word:

must must

Write the word:

Color the pizza slices that have the word "**must**"

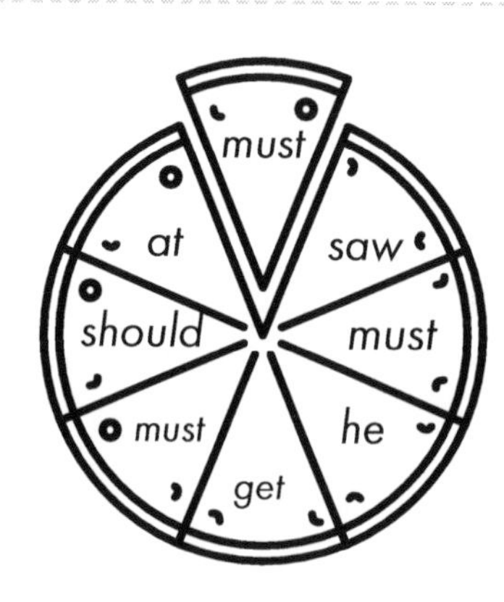

Let's work on our cutting and pasting skills. Cut out the word "**must**" from page 113 and paste it in the square box below to complete the sentence. Then read the sentence aloud!

You [ ] wear a jacket in the winter.

Write your own sentence using the word **must**:

My mom gave me a **new** computer.

Trace the word:

new new new

Write the word:

Color the puzzle pieces that have the word "**new**"

Find and circle the word "**new**"

w	o	f	o	p	l
j	a	w	e	n	v
h	o	r	r	t	o
p	c	w	e	e	l
w	n	l	w	e	a
v	j	x	f	d	x

Fill in the missing letters to make the word "**new**"

_ew n_w

_e_ __w

___ n__

My mom gave me a _ _ _ computer.

Write your own sentence using the word **new**:

There is **no** thunder today.

Trace the word:

no no no no

Write the word:

Color the puzzle pieces that have the word "**no**"

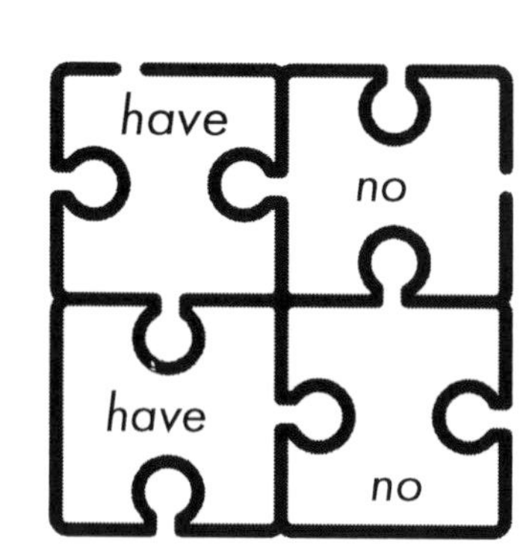

Let's work on our cutting and pasting skills. Cut out the word "**no**" from page 113 and paste it in the square box below to complete the sentence. Then read the sentence aloud!

There is [ ] thunder today.

Write your own sentence using the word **no**:

Can I go to the zoo **now**?

Trace the word:

Write the word:

Color the pizza slices that have the word "**now**"

Find and circle the word "**now**"

f	j	u	b	w	d
a	v	c	o	v	y
q	n	n	f	r	q
b	c	r	x	r	k
q	r	q	c	f	h
w	e	y	l	o	y

Fill in the missing letters to make the word "**now**"

_ow **n_w**

_o_ **__w**

___ **n__**

Can I go to the zoo _ _ _?

Write your own sentence using the word **now**:

I play soccer **on** Sundays.

Trace the word:

on on on on

Write the word:

Color the stars that have the word "**on**"

Let's work on our cutting and pasting skills. Cut out the word "**on**" from page 113 and paste it in the square box below to complete the sentence. Then read the sentence aloud!

I play soccer [ ] Sundays.

Write your own sentence using the word **on**:

Jamie wants to come to **our** party.

Trace the word:

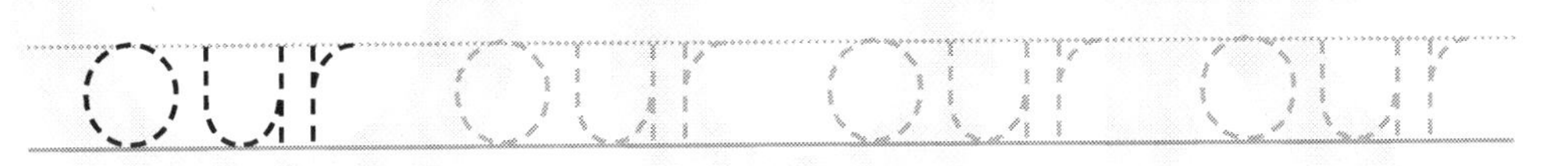

Write the word:

Color the pie pieces that have the word "**our**"

Find and circle the word "**our**"

z	h	o	s	v	x
h	u	p	s	z	h
r	d	n	g	l	a
f	p	m	b	x	c
h	o	u	x	a	i
z	z	y	m	a	l

Fill in the missing letters to make the word "**our**"

_ur **o_r** **_u_**

__r **___** **o__**

o__ **___** **___**

Jamie wants to come to _ _ _ party.

Write your own sentence using the word **our**:

The bedroom lights are **out**.

Trace the word:

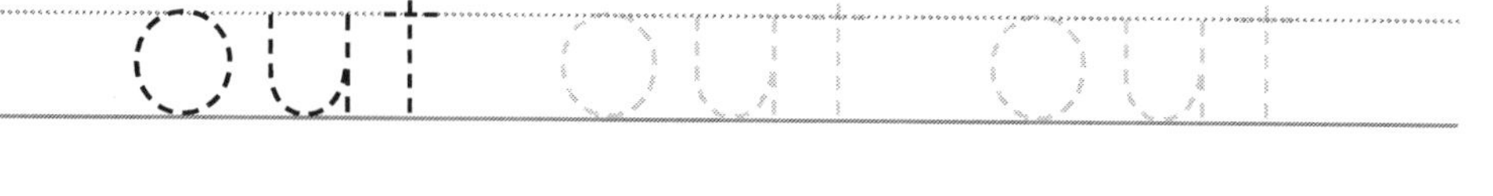

Write the word:

Color the pizza slices that have the word "**out**"

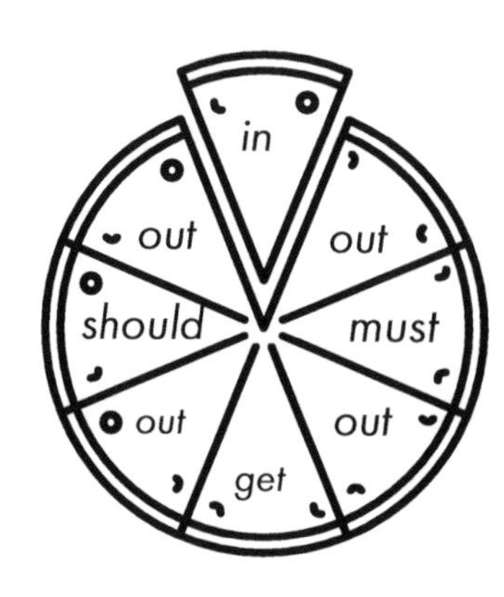

Let's work on our cutting and pasting skills. Cut out the word "**out**" from page 113 and paste it in the square box below to complete the sentence. Then read the sentence aloud!

The bedroom lights are [ ] .

Write your own sentence using the word **out**:

Can we **please** go outside?

Trace the word:

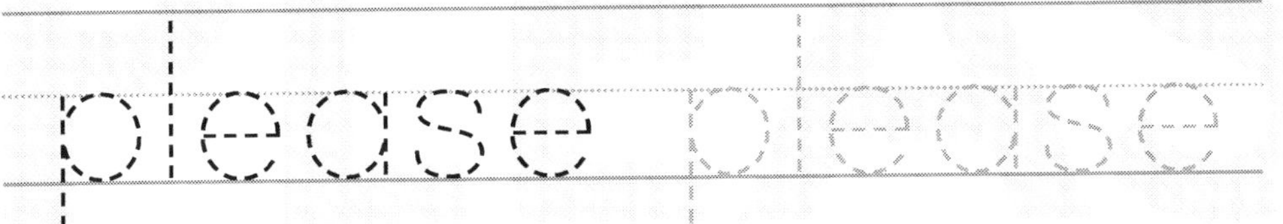

Write the word:

Color the puzzle pieces that have the word "**please**"

Find and circle the word "**please**"

y	w	e	k	o	i
z	j	s	q	i	u
a	q	a	o	o	q
p	o	e	b	s	v
c	l	l	b	n	v
w	f	p	b	j	t

Fill in the missing letters to make the word "**please**"

__ease p_e_s_

____se _l_a_e

______ _____e

Can we ______ go outside?

Write your own sentence using the word **please**:

That dress is **pretty**!

Trace the word:

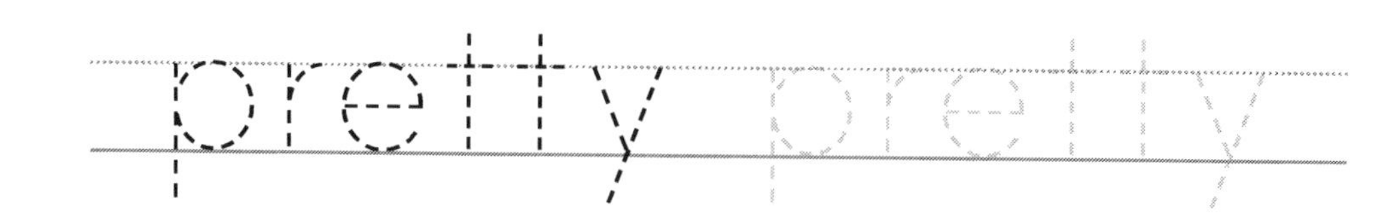

Write the word:

Color the puzzle pieces that have the word "**pretty**"

Let's work on our cutting and pasting skills. Cut out the word "**pretty**" from page 113 and paste it in the square box below to complete the sentence. Then read the sentence aloud!

This dress is [ ] .

Write your own sentence using the word **pretty**:

She **ran** to catch the bus.

Trace the word:

ran ran ran

Write the word:

Color the pizza slices that have the word "**ran**"

Find and circle the word "**ran**"

o p j j m e
t z r u n z
u h q y e l
m a o a c g
q m t k l s
r a n k p m

Fill in the missing letters to make the word "**ran**"

_an r_n

_a_ __n

___ r__

She ___ to catch the bus.

Write your own sentence using the word **ran**:

I **ride** my bike to school.

Trace the word:

Write the word:

Color the stars that have the word "**ride**"

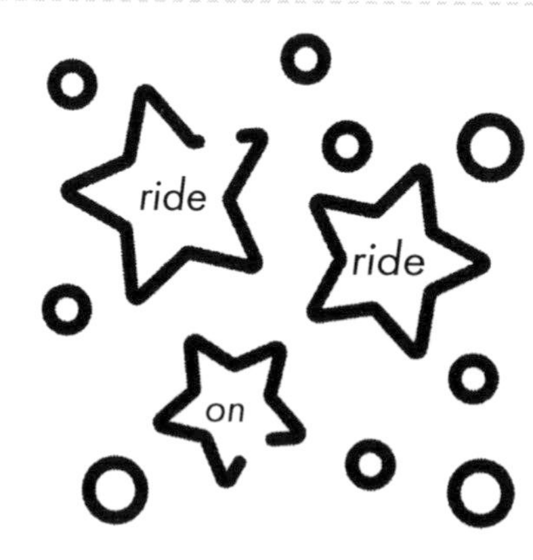

Let's work on our cutting and pasting skills. Cut out the word "**ride**" from page 113 and paste it in the square box below to complete the sentence. Then read the sentence aloud!

I [ ] my bike to school.

Write your own sentence using the word **ride**:

I **saw** a plane fly in the air.

Trace the word:

saw saw saw

Write the word:

Color the pie pieces that have the word "**saw**"

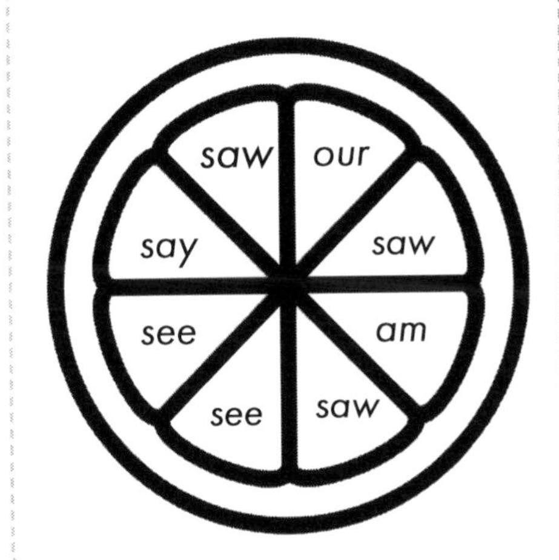

Find and circle the word "**saw**"

g h x k s g
l v p j g l
b j b s e p
y k d r g j
d g x j i h
f o y s e e

Fill in the missing letters to make the word "**saw**"

_aw s_w

_a_ __w

___ s__ ___

I ___ a plane fly in the air.

Write your own sentence using the word **saw**:

Say cheese!

Trace the word:

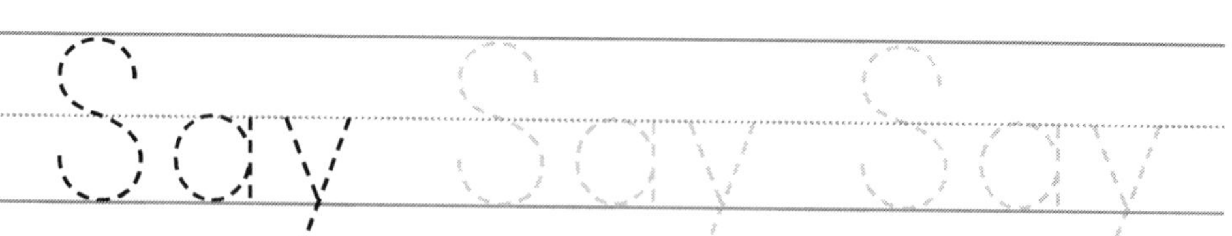

Write the word:

Color the pizza slices that have the word "**Say**"

Let's work on our cutting and pasting skills. Cut out the word "**Say**" from page 115 and paste it in the square box below to complete the sentence. Then read the sentence aloud!

Write your own sentence using the word **say**:

She wants to eat.

Trace the word:

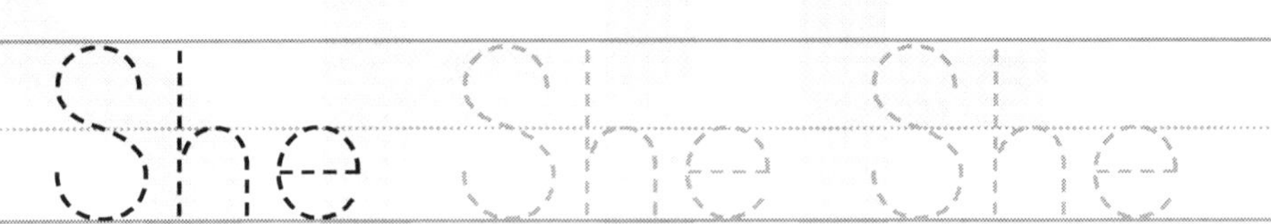

Write the word:

Color the puzzle pieces that have the word "**She**"

Find and circle the word "**She**"

s	r	l	p	l	z
j	h	s	a	b	e
n	a	e	a	l	h
h	v	o	q	m	s
v	i	x	d	y	h
i	x	j	w	k	s

Fill in the missing letters to make the word "**She**"

_he S_e _h_

__e ___ Sh_

___ ___ ___

___ wants to eat.

Write your own sentence using the word **she**:

I am **so** full!

Trace the word:

so so so so

Write the word:

Color the puzzle pieces that have the word "**so**"

Let's work on our cutting and pasting skills. Cut out the word "**so**" from page 115 and paste it in the square box below to complete the sentence. Then read the sentence aloud!

Write your own sentence using the word **so**:

Can we leave **soon**?

Trace the word:

soon soon

Write the word:

Color the pizza slices that have the word "**soon**"

Find and circle the word "**soon**"

d	s	u	r	t	y
s	o	f	n	p	c
n	o	r	h	t	h
b	n	g	t	y	m
x	h	b	l	m	j
t	k	o	o	z	u

Fill in the missing letters to make the word "**soon**"

_oon **s_on**

__on **_o_n**

s__n **____**

Can we leave _ _ _ _?

Write your own sentence using the word **soon**:

That is a rocket.

Trace the word:

That That That

Write the word:

Color the star that has the word "**That**"

Let's work on our cutting and pasting skills. Cut out the word "**That**" from page 115 and paste it in the square box below to complete the sentence. Then read the sentence aloud!

Write your own sentence using the word **that**:

There is a hole in this sock.

Trace the word:

There There

Write the word:

Color the pie pieces that have the word "**There**"

Find and circle the word "**There**"

u s b o o m
s w z f n l
m o h g z n
t h e r e g
w x o w e s
g u o f v b

Fill in the missing letters to make the word "**There**"

_here T_e_e

___re T__r_

_he__ _____

_ _ _ _ _ is a hole in this sock.

Write your own sentence using the word **there**:

They want to take the train.

Trace the word:

They They

Write the word:

Color the pizza slices that have the word "**They**"

Let's work on our cutting and pasting skills. Cut out the word "**They**" from page 115 and paste it in the square box below to complete the sentence. Then read the sentence aloud!

want to take the train.

Write your own sentence using the word **they**:

This is my notebook.

Trace the word:

This This This

Write the word:

Color the puzzle pieces that have the word "**This**"

Find and circle the word "**This**"

b	q	v	w	k	i
u	c	m	x	v	v
w	i	l	s	r	n
a	p	i	u	u	q
p	h	g	f	b	h
t	q	z	l	k	u

Fill in the missing letters to make the word "**This**"

_his T_i_ __is

Th__ _h__ T__s

___s ____ T___

____ is my notebook.

Write your own sentence using the word **this**:

I am **too** tired to exercise.

Trace the word:

too too too

Write the word:

Color the puzzle pieces that have the word "**too**"

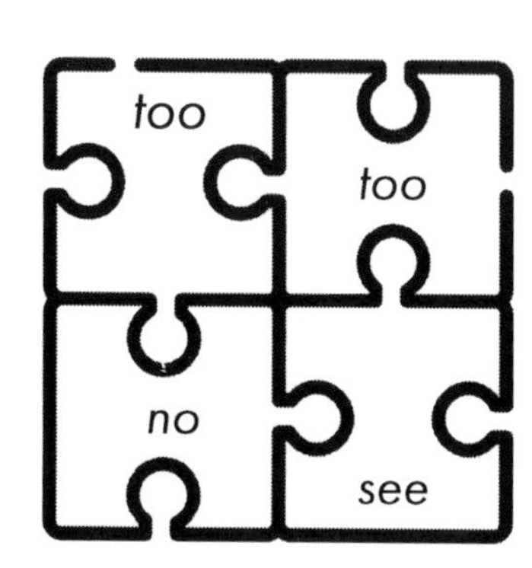

Let's work on our cutting and pasting skills. Cut out the word "**too**" from page 115 and paste it in the square box below to complete the sentence. Then read the sentence aloud!

I am [ ] tired to exercise.

Write your own sentence using the word **too**:

The pencil is **under** the table.

Trace the word:

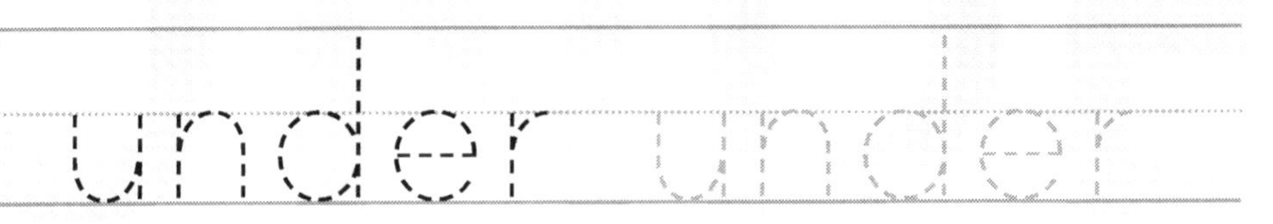

Write the word:

Color the pizza slices that have the word "**under**"

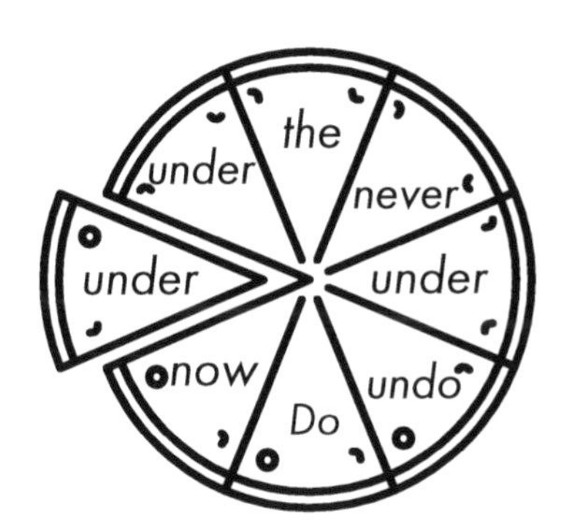

Find and circle the word "**under**"

e	y	c	k	r	v
o	b	u	l	y	u
f	t	q	g	u	n
m	g	e	z	h	d
a	u	n	t	n	e
w	f	i	e	d	r

Fill in the missing letters to make the word "**under**"

_nder **u_d_r**

___er **_n_e_**

u__e_ **_____**

The pencil is _____ the table.

Write your own sentence using the word **under**:

Do you **want** to visit Italy?

Trace the word:

want want want

Write the word:

Color the stars that have the word "**want**"

Let's work on our cutting and pasting skills. Cut out the word "**want**" from page 115 and paste it in the square box below to complete the sentence. Then read the sentence aloud!

Do you [ ] to visit Italy?

Write your own sentence using the word **want**:

John **was** excited for the trip.

Trace the word:

Write the word:

Color the pie pieces that have the word "**was**"

Find and circle the word "**was**"

u u e x i r
q r z a r j
r d e t z y
s a w t k j
z j m k h o
x k r k s h

Fill in the missing letters to make the word "**was**"

_as **w_s**

_a_ **__s**

___ **wa_**

John _ _ _ excited for the trip.

Write your own sentence using the word **was**:

She can sing very **well**.

Trace the word:

well well well

Write the word:

Color the pizza slices that have the word "**well**"

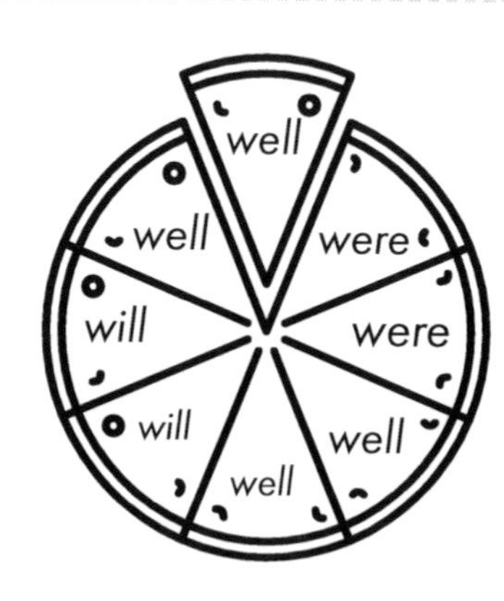

Let's work on our cutting and pasting skills. Cut out the word "**well**" from page 115 and paste it in the square box below to complete the sentence. Then read the sentence aloud!

She can sing very [ ] **.**

Write your own sentence using the word **well**:

Robert **went** to the dentist.

Trace the word:

Write the word:

Color the puzzle pieces that have the word "**went**"

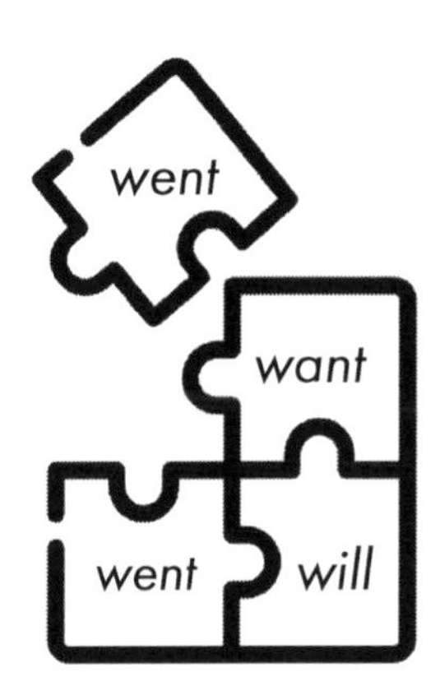

Find and circle the word "**went**"

y	k	u	c	p	b
h	i	y	x	y	y
t	b	g	y	w	c
b	k	j	j	e	y
b	v	x	p	n	h
p	i	j	z	t	s

Fill in the missing letters to make the word "**went**"

_ent w_n_ __nt

we__ _e__ w__t

___t ____ w___

Robert _ _ _ _ to the dentist.

Write your own sentence using the word **went**:

What time is it?

Trace the word:

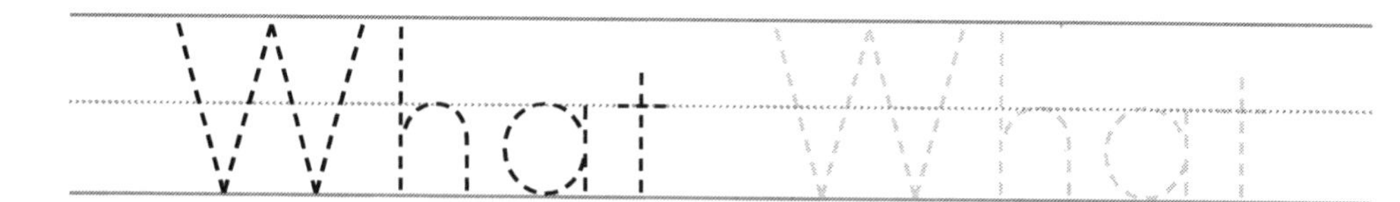

Write the word:

Color the puzzle pieces that have the word "**What**"

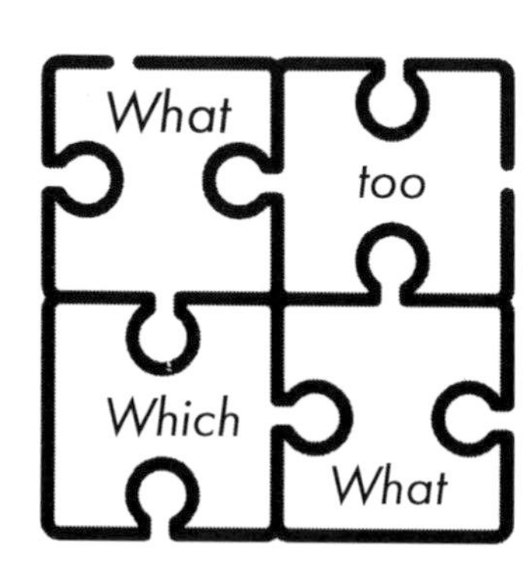

Let's work on our cutting and pasting skills. Cut out the word "**What**" from page 115 and paste it in the square box below to complete the sentence. Then read the sentence aloud!

Write your own sentence using the word **what**:

The bedroom ceiling is **white**.

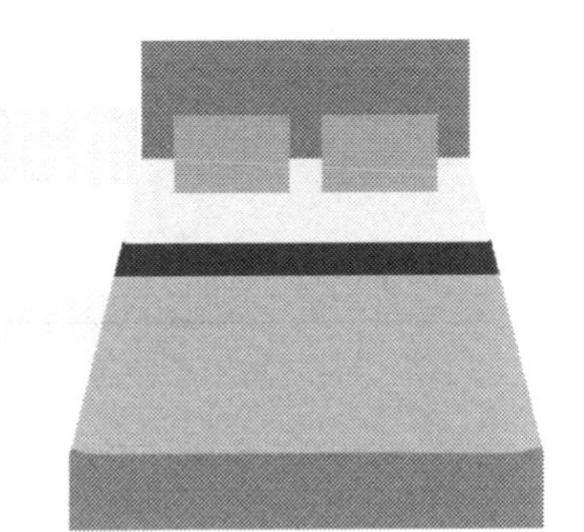

Trace the word:

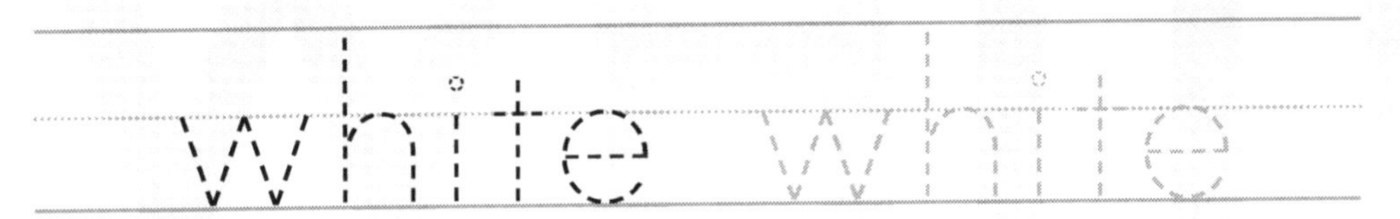

Write the word:

Color the pizza slices that have the word "**white**"

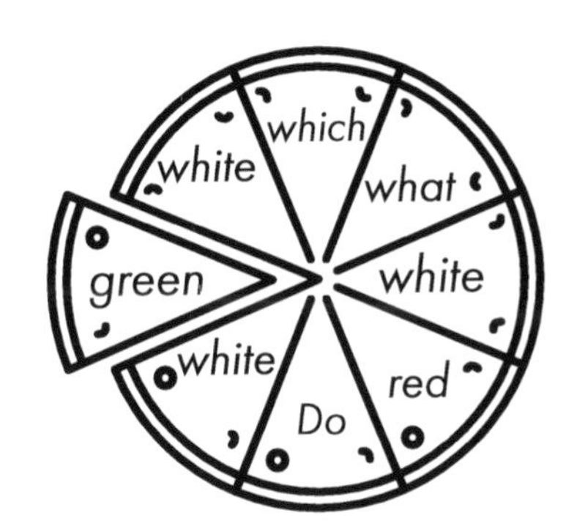

Find and circle the word "**white**"

b	t	b	t	b	p
b	i	w	s	i	b
w	h	i	t	e	k
e	e	i	p	w	i
e	h	e	k	b	h
n	r	q	r	m	x

Fill in the missing letters to make the word "**white**"

_hite w_i_e

___te _h_t_

w__t_ _____

The bedroom ceiling is _ _ _ _ _.

Write your own sentence using the word **white**:

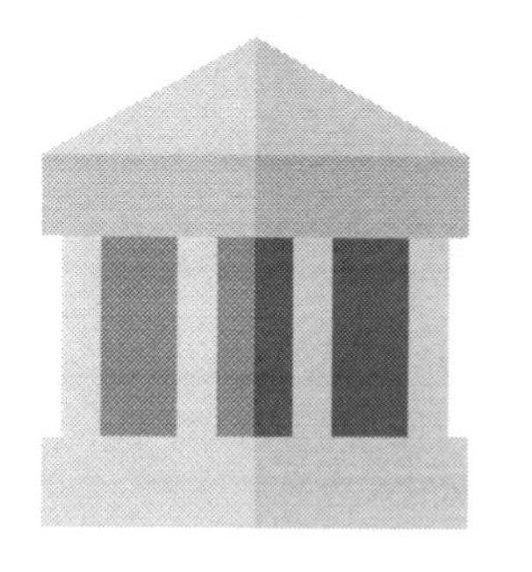

Who is coming to the museum?

Trace the word:

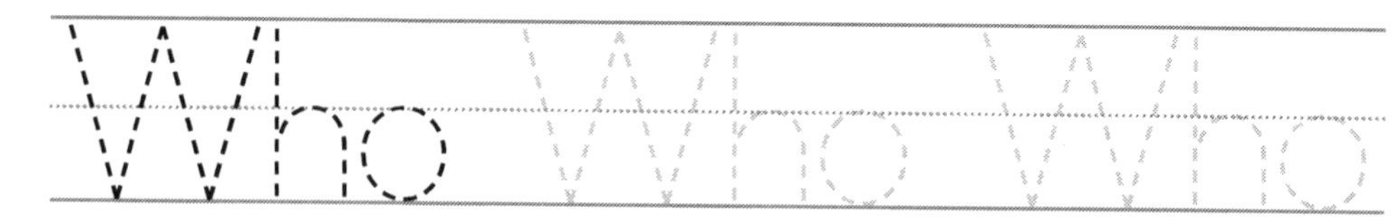

Write the word:

Color the star that has the word "**Who**"

Let's work on our cutting and pasting skills. Cut out the word "**Who**" from page 115 and paste it in the square box below to complete the sentence. Then read the sentence aloud!

[ ] is coming to the museum?

Write your own sentence using the word **who**:

Will you help me?

Trace the word:

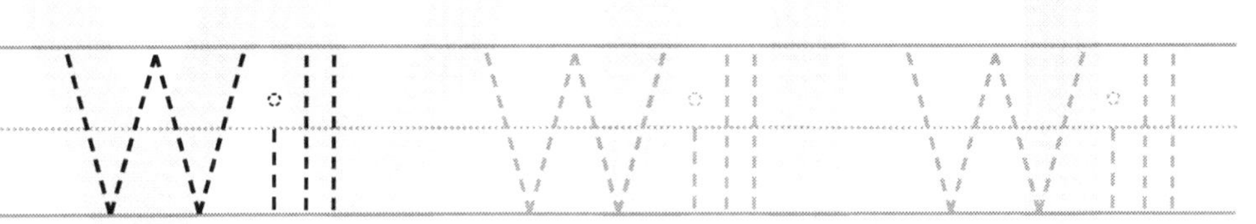

Write the word:

Color the pie pieces that have the word "**Will**"

Find and circle the word "**Will**"

y q x q o k
j f l y x u
i y l h y h
d y i q n s
n y w q m c
u q y m v n

Fill in the missing letters to make the word "**Will**"

_ill **W_l_**

___l **_i_l**

_i__ **____**

____ you help me?

Write your own sentence using the word **will**:

I agree **with** you.

Trace the word:

with with with

Write the word:

Color the pizza slices that have the word "**with**"

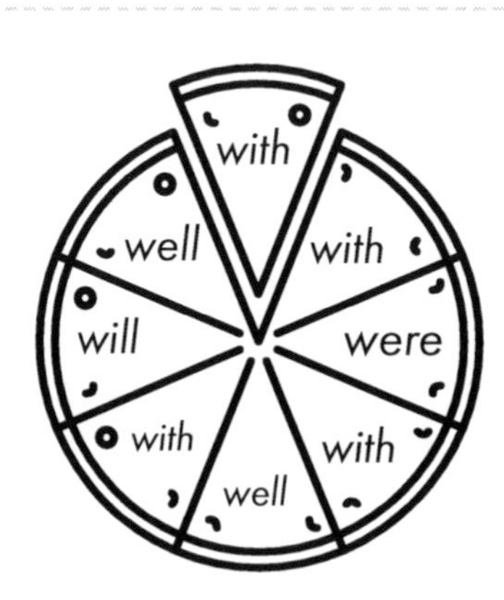

Let's work on our cutting and pasting skills. Cut out the word "**with**" from page 115 and paste it in the square box below to complete the sentence. Then read the sentence aloud!

I agree [ ] you.

Write your own sentence using the word **with**:

Yes, I got an A+.

Trace the word:

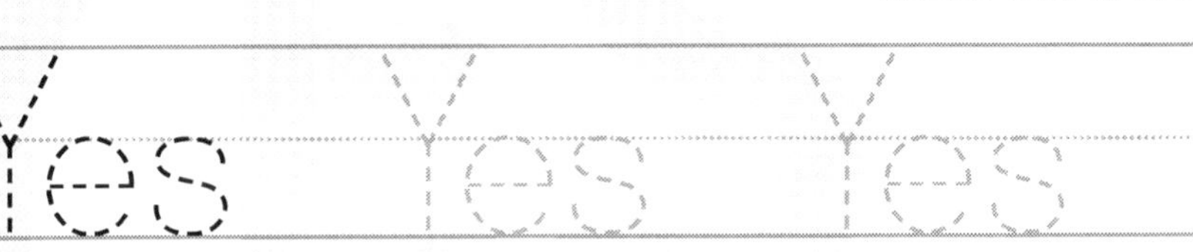

Write the word:

Color the puzzle pieces that have the word "**Yes**"

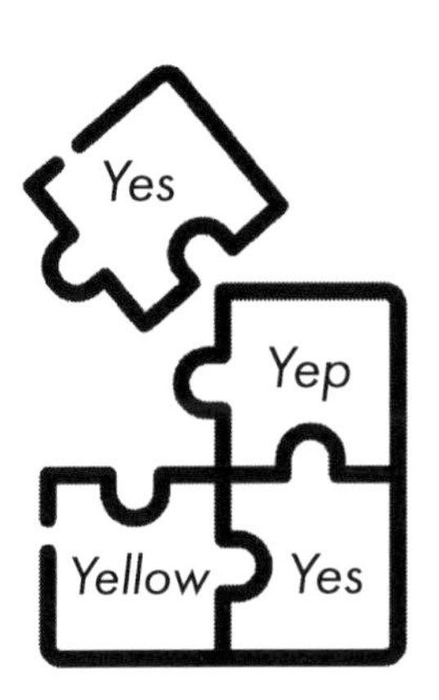

Find and circle the word "**Yes**"

y o y b m u
k e q p x w
s e q h t u
m e d r s w
z r g u u w
e v p p t a

Fill in the missing letters to make the word "**Yes**"

_es Y_s

_e_ __s

___ Ye_

___, I got an A+.

Write your own sentence using the word **Yes**:

I will eat **after** I finish my homework.

Trace the word:

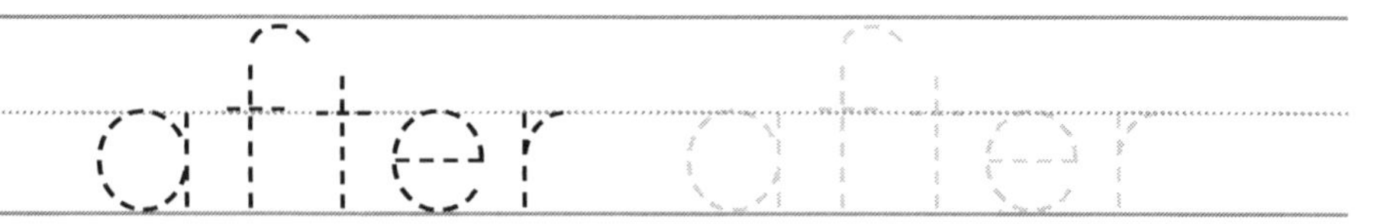

Write the word:

Color the puzzle pieces that have the word "**after**"

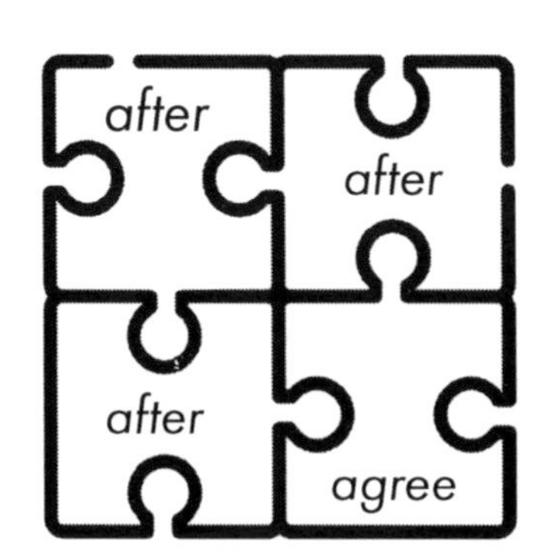

Let's work on our cutting and pasting skills. Cut out the word "**after**" from page 115 and paste it in the square box below to complete the sentence. Then read the sentence aloud!

I will eat [ ] I finish my homework.

Write your own sentence using the word **after**:

Can you repeat that **again**?

Trace the word:

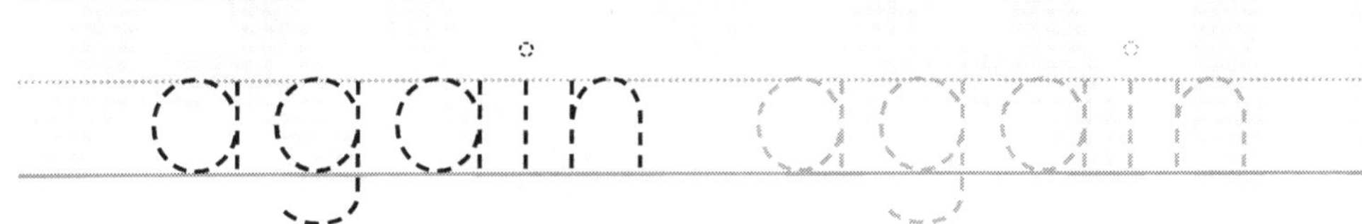

Write the word:

Color the pizza slices that have the word "**again**"

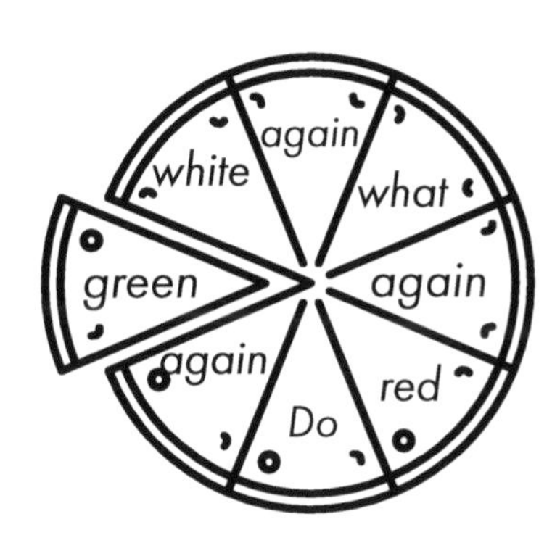

Find and circle the word "**again**"

k	r	o	n	a	l
x	c	j	u	g	t
g	w	n	f	a	e
n	s	l	k	i	h
b	q	m	p	n	w
d	g	p	g	z	v

Fill in the missing letters to make the word "**again**"

_gain **a_a_n**

___in **_g_i_**

a_a__ **_____**

Can you repeat that _ _ _ _ _?

Write your own sentence using the word **again**:

I have **an** idea.

Trace the word:

an an an an

Write the word:

Color the stars that have the word "**an**"

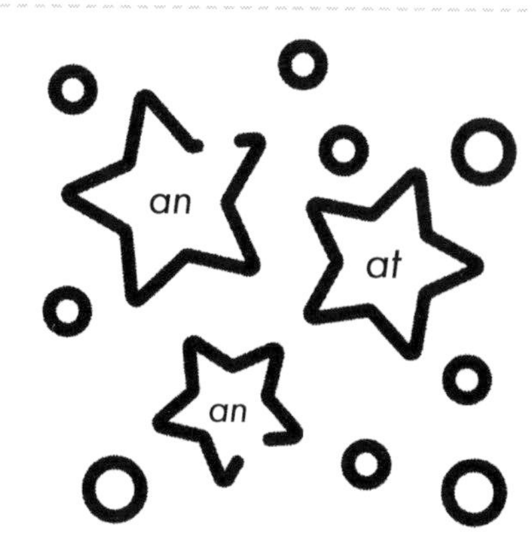

Let's work on our cutting and pasting skills. Cut out the word "**an**" from page 115 and paste it in the square box below to complete the sentence. Then read the sentence aloud!

I have [ ] idea.

Write your own sentence using the word **an**:

There isn't **any** bread left.

Trace the word:

any any any

Write the word:

Color the pie pieces that have the word "**any**"

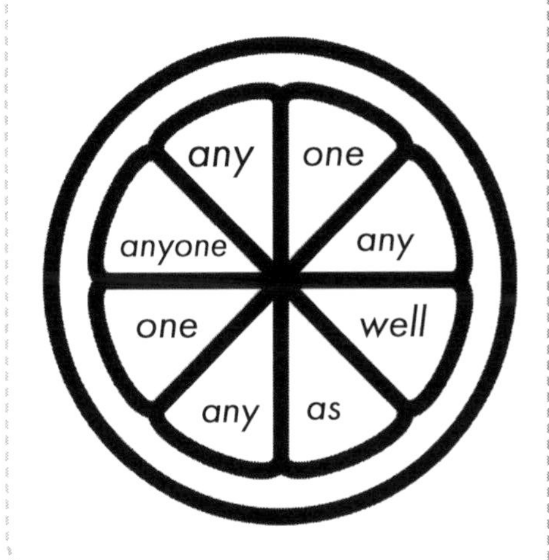

Find and circle the word "**any**"

y	b	r	o	r	i
q	r	m	r	u	y
x	g	h	m	n	n
l	w	i	k	q	a
x	t	w	i	w	c
m	d	w	v	f	h

Fill in the missing letters to make the word "**any**"

_ny **a_y**

a_y **_n_**

__y **___**

There isn't _ _ _ bread left.

Write your own sentence using the word **any**:

I'm busy **as** a bee.

Trace the word:

as as as as

Write the word:

Color the pizza slices that have the word "**as**"

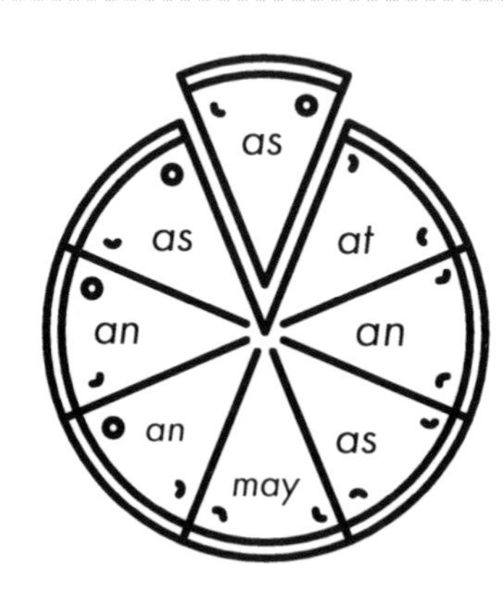

Let's work on our cutting and pasting skills. Cut out the word "**as**" from page 115 and paste it in the square box below to complete the sentence. Then read the sentence aloud!

I'm busy [ ] a bee.

Write your own sentence using the word **as**:

Can I **ask** a question?

Trace the word:

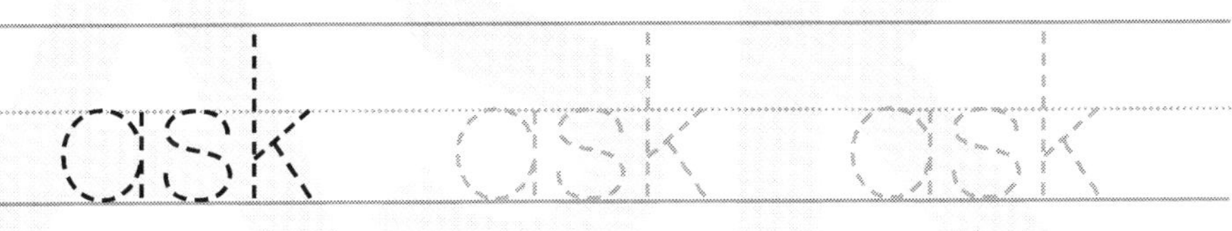

Write the word:

Color the puzzle pieces that have the word "**ask**"

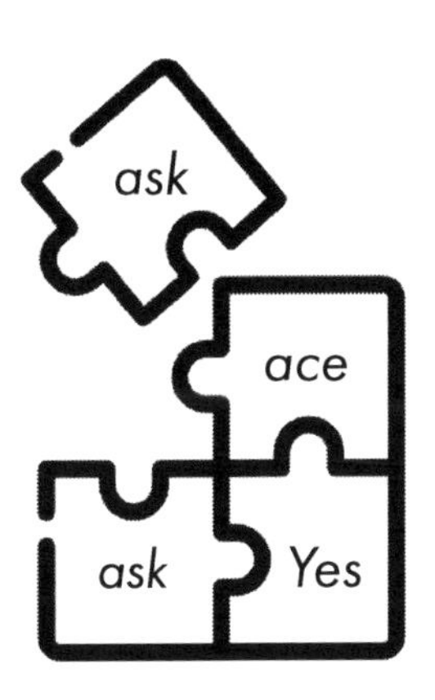

Find and circle the word "**ask**"

c	f	l	s	t	j
y	p	g	p	d	n
l	p	y	e	l	x
a	s	k	i	i	j
g	z	j	g	t	l
m	a	m	e	o	c

Fill in the missing letters to make the word "**ask**"

_sk **a_k**

_s_ **__k**

___ **as_**

Can I _ _ _ a question?

Write your own sentence using the word **ask**:

I need to be home **by** seven.

Trace the word:

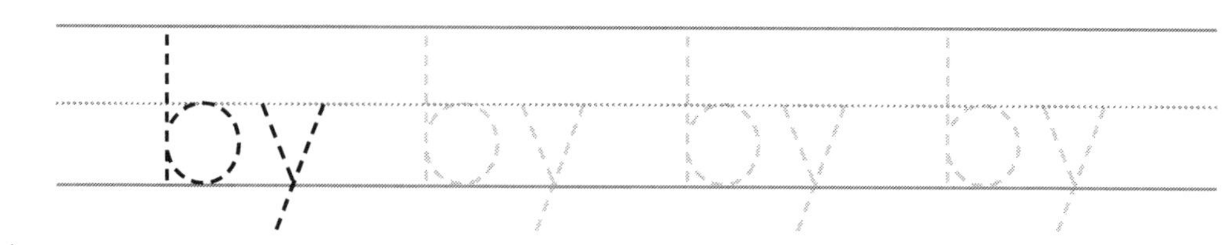

Write the word:

Color the puzzle pieces that have the word "**by**"

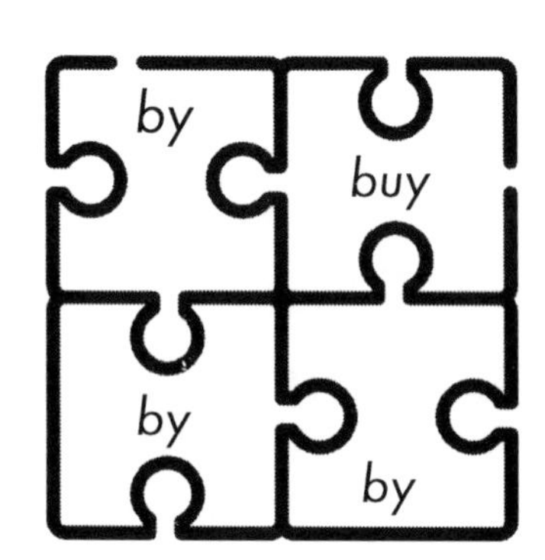

Let's work on our cutting and pasting skills. Cut out the word "**by**" from page 115 and paste it in the square box below to complete the sentence. Then read the sentence aloud!

I need to be home [ ] seven.

Write your own sentence using the word **by**:

I wish I **could** swim.

Trace the word:

could could

Write the word:

Color the pizza slices that have the word "**could**"

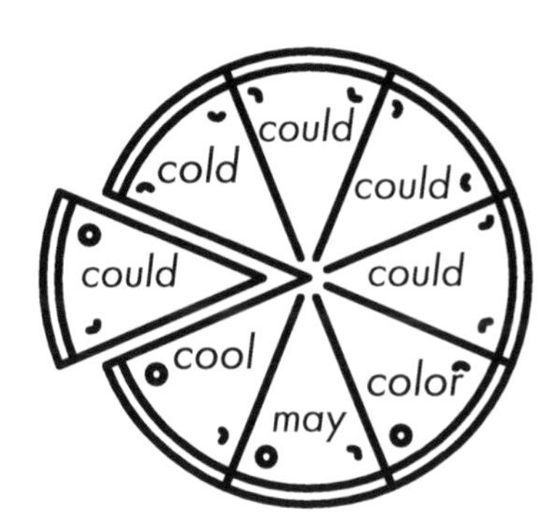

Find and circle the word "**could**"

q o s f d d
r u e l c m
l e u h o n
e o y y p s
c m g f i e
j k j k b k

Fill in the missing letters to make the word "**could**"

_ould c_u_d

___ld _o_l_

c_u__ _____

I wish I _ _ _ _ _ swim.

Write your own sentence using the word **could**:

ARGOPREP
PRE-SCHOOL

CUT & PASTE

Instructions:

Locate the correct sight words and cut out the words carefully!
Paste the sight words into the corresponding pages.

ARGOPREP
PRE-SCHOOL

Instructions:

Locate the correct sight words and cut out the words carefully!
Paste the sight words into the corresponding pages.

a | away | blue | I

come | need | funny

help | jump | is | Look

not | me | run | see

two | play | three

yellow | all | We

ate | black | are

ARGOPREP
PRE-SCHOOL

Instructions:

Locate the correct sight words and cut out the words carefully!
Paste the sight words into the corresponding pages.

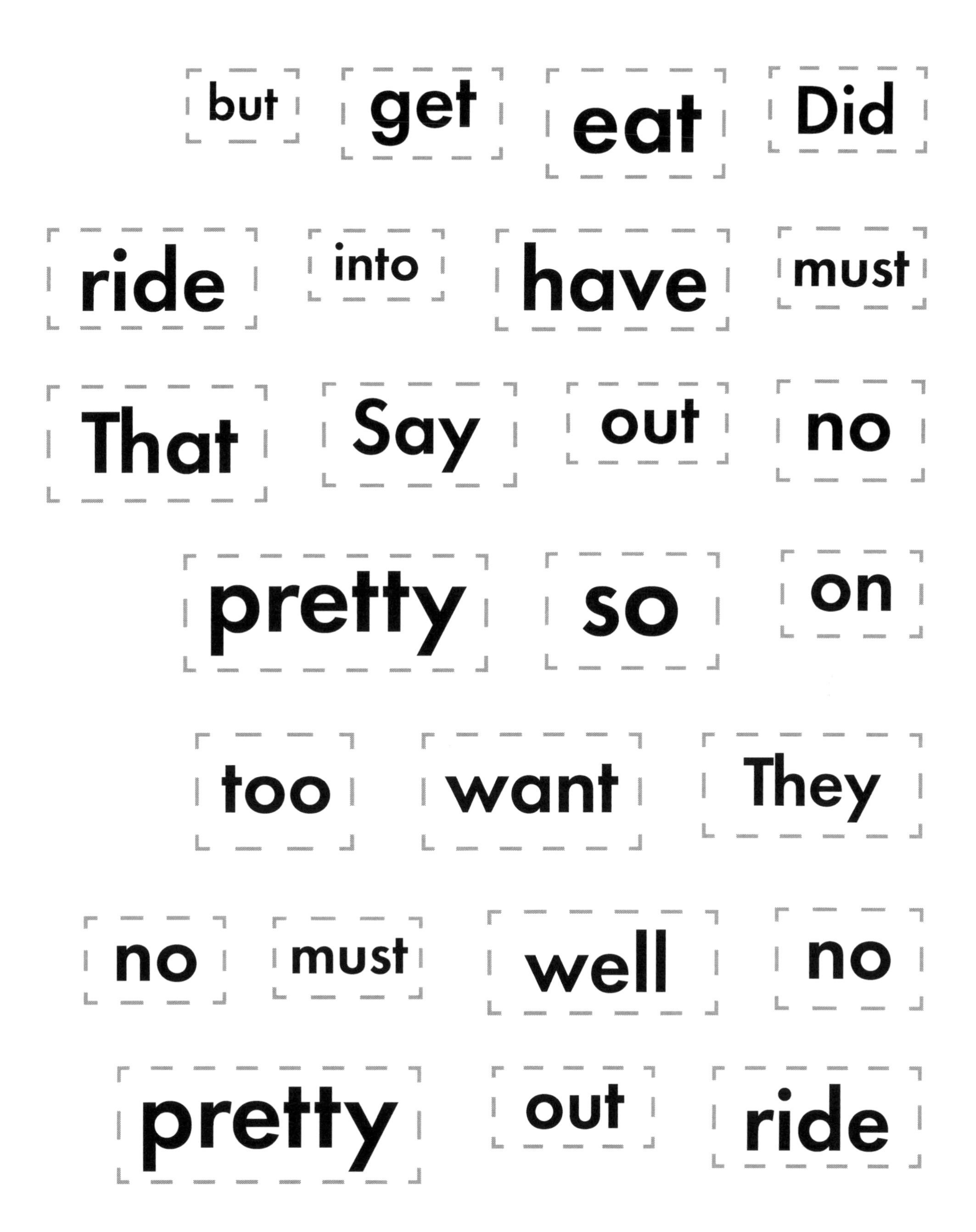

ARGOPREP
PRE-SCHOOL

Instructions:

Locate the correct sight words and cut out the words carefully!
Paste the sight words into the corresponding pages.

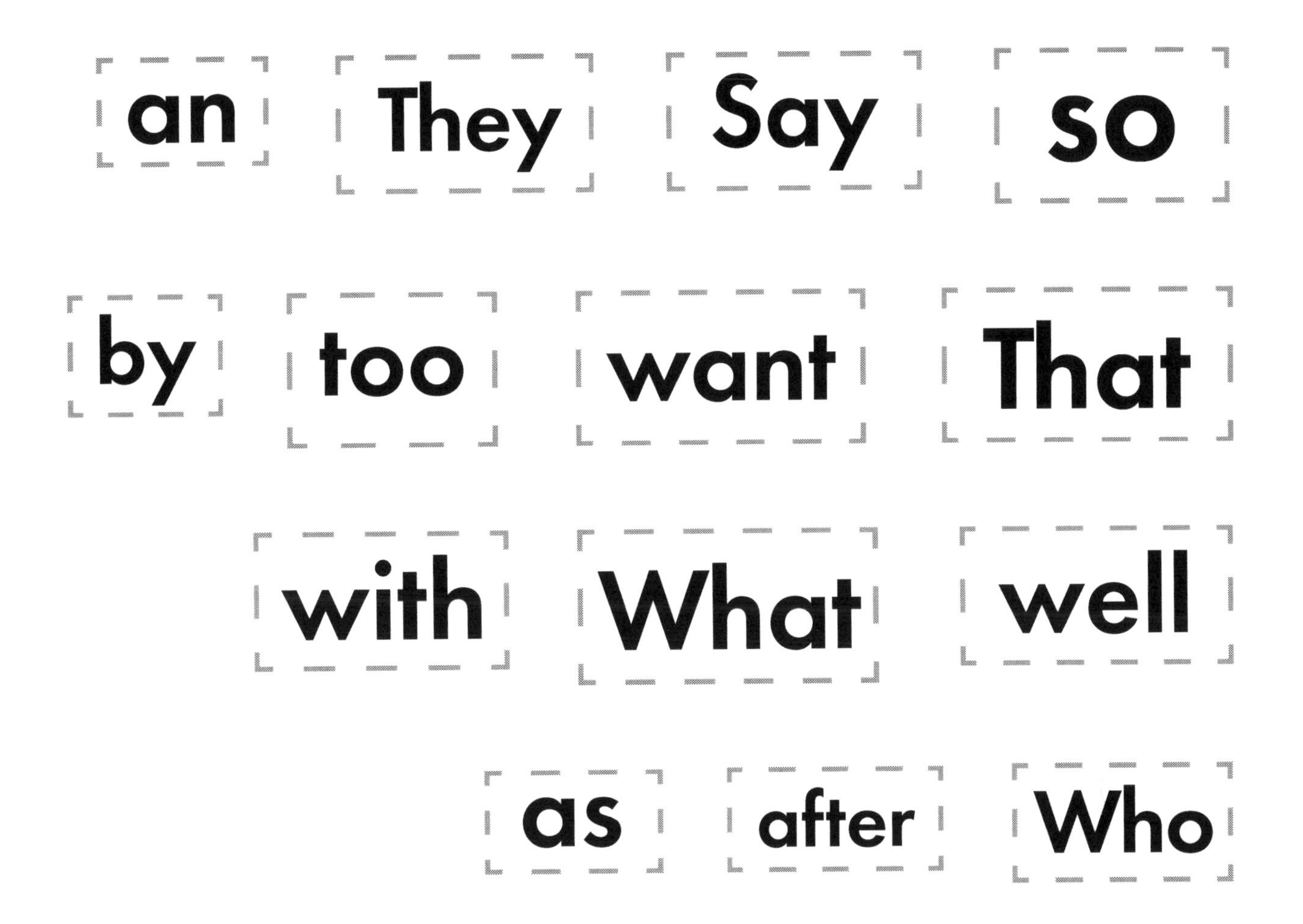

Made in the USA
Lexington, KY
20 January 2019